THE NON-LINEAR MIND

The Non-Linear Mind is one of a series of low-cost books under the title PSYCHOANALYTIC IDEAS which brings together the best of public lectures and other writings given by analysts of the British Psycho-Analytical Society on important psychoanalytic subjects.

Series Editor: James Rose

Recent titles in the Psychoanalytic Ideas Series
(for a full listing, please visit www.karnacbooks.com)

THE NON-LINEAR MIND

Psychoanalyis of Complexity in Psychic Life

edited by

*James Rose and
Graham Shulman*

KARNAC

First published in 2016 by
Karnac Books Ltd
118 Finchley Road, London NW3 5HT

British Library Cataloguing in Publication Data

A C.I.P. for this book is available from the British Library

ISBN 978 1 78220 433 6

Edited, designed and produced by The Studio Publishing Services Ltd
www.publishingservicesuk.co.uk
email: studio@publishingservicesuk.co.uk

Printed in Great Britain

www.karnacbooks.com

CONTENTS

ACKNOWLEDGEMENTS

A special thanks to all our colleagues and friends who have helped us to structure our thoughts and consolidate our ideas. They have given generously of their time and their knowledge. We have been touched by the way in which they have responded to this project.

Thanks must also go to Taylor & Francis Ltd and Wiley Ltd for their kind permission to use previously published material in this book.

Finally, we would like to thank our families, who have endured our preoccupation with extremely good grace. Without them this book would not have been possible.

ABOUT THE EDITORS AND CONTRIBUTORS

Robert Galatzer-Levy is Clinical Professor of Psychiatry and Behavioral Neurosciences at the University of Chicago. He has published extensively on the conceptual links between theories of complexity and psychoanalysis.

George Moran was Director of the Anna Freud Centre from 1987 until his death in 1991. He is remembered as a man with a lively intelligence and diverse interests. He made ground-breaking contributions to the psychological understanding of children who developed brittle diabetes, thereby showing his belief that a sound psychology could not be practised in isolation from other disciplines.

James Rose is a Fellow of the British Psychoanalytical Society. He is a former chair of the British Psychoanalytic Council, which is the regulator for psychoanalytic psychotherapy in the UK. Currently, he has a private psychoanalytic practice in London. He is the editor of the Psychoanalytic Ideas series published by Karnac.

Graham Shulman is a consultant child and adolescent psychotherapist and Head of Child Psychotherapy in CAMHS, NHS Lanarkshire. He was previously an Editor of the *Journal of Child Psychotherapy*. He has published a number of articles and chapters on clinical work and on psychoanalysis and literature. He is currently an Assistant Editor of the *Journal of Infant Observation*.

Paul Whittle was a lecturer in the Department of Experimental Psychology at Cambridge University and researched extensively in vision. He also had a long-standing interest in psychoanalysis and was concerned about what he saw as an ever widening gulf between psychoanalysis as a therapy and psychology as a scientific discipline. He died in 2009.

Introduction

This book is concerned with whether we can develop our understanding of the mind through the application of new approaches to the study of complex systems. It is titled *The Non-linear Mind* because of the daily observation that the mind is complex and complex systems are essentially non-linear. What this means is that they cannot be adequately modelled mathematically using linear equations. In practical terms, this means that the accurate prediction of a response to any one stimulus becomes difficult, if not impossible. This is often because these systems exist in the world as entities that are in a dynamic relation with their environments. In the case of *living* dynamical systems (or living organisms), they must be adaptive in their responses to maintain their integrity. This relies upon accurate perception of their environment at any one time. In a very real way, they must be alive to changes in their environment if they are to stay viable by responding appropriately.

However, the scope of the study of complex systems does not confine itself to living organisms. An example is the weather system: the problems of its prediction are of concern, if not to say interest, to all of us. Some might feel that the weather can be a bit of a bore, usually because it is so unpredictable and uncontrollable, but the fact remains that it poses a problem. This is because it is complex, that is, has many contributory causes, is in a constant state of flux, and cannot be easily forecast.

In recent years, the study of complexity has led to the development of what has come to be known as chaos theory. Chaos theory has been a conceptual response to the practical difficulties encountered when trying to predict the behaviour of what are thought of as complex systems. Chaos theory studies the behaviour of dynamical systems that are highly sensitive to initial conditions, an effect which is popularly referred to as the "butterfly effect". Small differences in initial conditions (such as those due to rounding errors in numerical computation) can yield widely diverging outcomes for such dynamical systems, rendering long-term prediction impossible in general. This happens even if these systems are internally structured, meaning that their future behaviour is fully determined when random external factors are ignored, which can never be the case. In other words, the deterministic nature of these systems does not make them predictable so far as their manifest behaviour is concerned , unlike linear systems. This behaviour is known as deterministic chaos, or simply chaos.

When the human mind began to be studied in a systematic way in the nineteenth century, it is hardly surprising that the means of investigation devised were strongly influenced by the structure of the methods that had been developed for the study of natural phenomena. What was studied was heavily influenced by *what* it was that it was thought possible to study and *how* it was possible to study it. In trying to relate one variable to another, variables had to be capable of being measured reliably and validly. Thus, the means of measurement had to be able to demonstrate that two measurements of the same thing taken in succession would give the same result: that is, that it could be said to be a reliable measure. Further, the measures had to be able to show that they indeed measured what they claimed to measure, that is, that they were valid.

These were the requirements of data to be entered into the predominant mathematical equations then in use for researching the relationship between variables. These were linear differential equations. However, many people were frustrated by the limitations imposed by these requirements placed upon the matters that could be researched. It is not surprising that this was reflected in a split that went far beyond the study of the human mind. This split is described by Paul Whittle in Chapter Two. It tends to be a split in so far as the adherents of one side of the split have looked at the other with some contempt and asked themselves and their opponents, "How can you think like that?" It is reminiscent of the split described by British scientist and novelist C. P. Snow in part of his influential 1959 Rede Lecture in his division between the arts and sciences, also known as what he called "the two cultures" (Snow, 1961).

So, a question was posed for those interested in studying that quintessentially non-linear system—the mind. How are we to be objective in studying subjectivity? First of all, the mind is staggeringly complex and unpredictable. After all, it evolved in response to the requirement to be able to survive in complex and unpredictable conditions. Second, from the point of view of those studying it, it has the irritating property of reacting to being studied. In other words, it both behaves and experiences. Some might say that it might be best to leave well alone and avoid studying something upon which we cannot put conceptual spanners.

The trouble with this position is that we have no choice but to study ourselves because we are probably the biggest threat to our survival as a species. There is the conceivable position that to cease this enquiry could be suicidal—in short, we would be mad to give up on ourselves as an object of study. So, the question is, how are we to do it? It is this dilemma that led some psychoanalysts to consider the conceptual possibilities offered by chaos theory to help address the problems of thinking about how to study the mind. This is because the mind is described more accurately by a non-linear model.

An important reason for the appeal of chaos theory to some psychoanalysts is that the phenomena to which it applies and its method of study bear a striking resemblance to the psychoanalytic theory and method developed by Freud. Essentially, the psychoanalytic method of investigation is based upon creating an iterating learning system. It iterates in that the product of the first meeting of the psychoanalyst with an analysand feeds forward into the next, and so on. Over time, patterns of behaviour and affect become observable to both parties in the system: the psychoanalyst and the analysand (aka the patient). If the analysis is properly conducted, what emerges are the characteristic properties of the analysand's anxieties, impulses, and defences that effectively control their lives and of which they might be only partly aware. It was out of this method of investigation that the components of Freud's model of the mind—anxieties, impulses and defences in all their non-linear complexity leading to the structural model—emerged. However, it is only in very recent years that some psychoanalysts have seen the potential links between the study of non-linear systems and the mind. This book is an attempt to consider some of the links that have been made and how they might develop in the future.

Looking at these links shows that another reason for the interest in chaos theory is that it offers the prospect of healing the split that Whittle identified, which is referred to above. This is because the method necessary for the investigation of experience assumes that it cannot be understood in the immediate. It is only over time that the *patterns* of experience can be observed within an iterative learning system. This enables us to deepen our understanding of the psychoanalytic process through the examination of the properties of iterative systems. The implication is that we are not forced by the unique quality of the analysis of any one person to treat it as a phenomenon that cannot be compared with another. While any one individual is unique, just as their analysis will be, this does not mean that the process by which the analysis is conducted is idiosyncratic and incomparable to other analytic experiences. By thinking about the mind, and the means of studying it, as being non-linear systems, we can do justice to the reality of the complexity of what we are studying. Further, we have an instrument—the psychoanalytic iterating learning system—which is, as it were, "fit for purpose" in the study of the mind's complexity.

Of course, the experience that psychoanalysts have gained from the work of psychoanalysis has enabled various generalisations to be made about the features of all human subjects. These are made manifest by the different theoretical approaches that have emerged over the past century but which can seem incompatible. However, ultimately, this book proposes that the study of the process of psychoanalytic investigation using the concepts derived from chaos theory offers the prospect of becoming more objective about the experience of subjectivity.

A central idea, in the study of non-linear complex dynamical systems, is the strange attractor. The very name of David Ruelle's

(1980) conceptual creation—the strange attractor—has, I think, intuitive appeal for all, even if the prospect of beginning to grasp it as a mathematical concept may seem, for some, too daunting. The strange attractor can seem to have a poetic appeal; Ruelle himself thought of it as being of psychoanalytic interest. I mention it now because the concept is continually referred to by the contributors to this book. An introduction to this concept is offered in Chapter One.

This book is divided into two parts. The first part consists of an introduction to the concept of non-linear systems and, particularly, the notion of the strange attractor, and then is concerned with the application of non-linear systems theory to the psychoanalytic study of the mind. It will be seen that the application of a non-linear model to understanding the structure and functioning of the mind has substantial implications. For example, processes of development can no longer be assumed to follow a linear succession suggested by the linear "arrow of time". This implies a radical rethinking of our understanding of psychic development as a response by the individual to their environment in all its forms. Thinking of the mind as a complex non-linear system has the potential for making links between the so-called empirical approach (which tends to think of brains) and the hermeneutic approaches (which prefer to think of minds). This reflects a deep philosophical split in the human sciences which has proved very difficult to bridge.

The second part of the book is concerned with the technical application of the ideas of chaos theory to the understanding of therapeutic action and psychic change. It concludes with a consideration of the research and clinical implications of considering the mind as a non-linear system. For example, thinking of the mind as a complex non-linear system has the potential to change our therapeutic focus from the subject-object relation to the analysis of characteristic situations between the two. In these situations, time and space cannot be assumed to be linear. This has the potential to free psychoanalysts from the methodological constraints imposed by the linear model with benefit for psychoanalysts and their patients alike. Advances in neuro-psychoanalysis have also offered new ways of healing the mind-brain split referred to above. This book may therefore be of interest to those who are interested in following up the implications of these new advances in thinking about how to be objective about subjectivity.

References

Ruelle, D. (1980). Strange attractors. *Mathematical Intelligencer*, 2: 126–137.
Snow, C. P. (1961). *The Two Cultures and the Scientific Revolution*. New York: Cambridge University Press.

PART I

THE APPLICATION OF NON-LINEAR DYNAMICAL SYSTEMS THEORY TO THE PSYCHOANALYTICAL STUDY OF THE MIND

Introduction to Part I

This part of the book comprises an initial chapter by James Rose introducing the concept of non-linear systems, with particular emphasis on the notion of the "strange attractor", followed by three chapters based on papers which are concerned with showing how non-linear systems theory can be relevant to understanding the workings of the human mind. At the heart of them is the proposal that studying and understanding the human mind requires a model that does justice to its fundamental property of non-linearity. The first paper (Chapter Two) looks at the situation that prevailed before the theory of complex systems had had much impact on psychoanalytical thinkers. It is by Paul Whittle and, essentially, he shows how investigators of the mind have divided into two apparently irreconcilable groups. Luyten et al. (2006) identified this split as the divide into the nomothetic approach and the ideographic one. The first approach sought to work through the consideration of the relation between the human and its environment through the study of behaviour in controlled conditions where systematic measurement could be achieved. Another method was to study individual differences where similar standards of reliable and valid measurement could be devised; for example, the study of individual differences in intelligence. These were called nomothetic because the accent was upon looking at *behaviour*.

Those pursuing an ideographic approach were more concerned with a person's *experience* and relied upon systematic case studies for their research design in the absence of the possibility of systematic measurement. The identification with the prevailing scientific method or against it defined the split. Whittle, an experimental psychologist, makes a plea for investigators of the mind to have a foot in both camps in order to find a way of healing this potentially destructive split.

This is followed by Moran's (1991) paper. He begins by saying that

> For many disciplines, the focus of study is a system that sometimes behaves predictably and, with a change in certain conditions, behaves in a complex or apparently random manner. In meteorology, fluid dynamics, and ecology, scientists have constructed models of their respective systems, attempting to capture the complex nature and behaviour seen in real life. Until the last ten or fifteen years, such models consisted of numerous equations which had to be "summed" in order to account for the variety possible in a real world system (this was true when trying to model even the simplest physical systems).
>
> Experimental observations that deviated from the models were considered artifactitious, or the deviations were resolved by the *addition* of more components or equations. Mathematical approaches to modelling have, for a number of years, examined systems that work on themselves over time, that "flow". This approach drops the previous notion of tag-on equations to encompass supposedly variant behaviour, and shows that complex behaviour can be determined by simple equations of a special class, called non-linear differential equations (May, 1976). Many systems that are so modelled work on themselves, or "flow": the old "output" becomes the new "input". This process of flow suggests images of fluids, and indeed it is in the discipline of fluid dynamics that much of the pioneering work has occurred. Such fluidic systems characterised by this kind of feedback are prone to exhibit "chaotic" behaviour over time: behaviour that is *apparently* random, disorganised, and without order. The science of these new models is in fact called "Chaos". The choice of the name is unfortunate, because there is little that is truly lawless, destructive, or totally disorderly about the field or its subjects of study. Indeed, the new models allow a clearer appreciation of qualitative and *quantitative* characteristics of complex systems never before possible.

Thus, Moran makes a case for the utility of the theory of what he calls dynamical systems theory for thinking about psychic processes and the mind as a whole.

This part of the book concludes with a paper by Galatzer-Levy (2004), who concerns himself with the idea of development, which is a central idea for psychoanalysts. He avers that an epigenetic assumption pervades psychoanalytic thinking about development, psychic or physical. By this, he meant that the organism acquires its complexity because of what is effectively a kind of programme which is intrinsic to that organism from birth. In this view, there is an assumption, which he calls the epigenetic assumption, that normal development may be thought of as an orderly sequence. Disorder is seen as predictive of pathology. However, what is observed is something quite different in that normal development is characterised by discontinuity, which is not predicted by the epigenetic assumption (see Emde & Spicer, 2000). Abandoning this view prepares us to see a great deal more about the development of an individual than the epigenetic view will allow. How an individual develops will be a function of his potential from birth, but how he turns out will be a function of the impact of external factors and how they have been experienced.

Further, we can assume that these patterns, which are developed by the individual as she learns to live in the world, reflect her history, the kinds of anxieties she has faced, and what it was that it seemed to her that she had to do in order to survive psychically and physically. Because they concern psychic survival, they will not be given up easily without anxiety. Efforts to do this by persuasion or appeal to common sense by a third party will inevitably fail, particularly if all that is achieved by these appeals is compliance to what is experienced as a terrifying third party because they will appear to threaten their survival. Thus, thinking in this way changes our perspective of the individual from something that reacts to stimuli to one that emphasises that the individual actively and idiosyncratically engages with his world—internal and external—in a manner that truly reflects the non-linear property of his mind.

References

Emde, R. N., & Spicer, P. (2000). Experience in the midst of variation: new horizons for development and psychopathology. *Development and Psychopathology, 12*: 313–331.

Luyten, P., Blatt, S. J., & Corveleyn, J. (2006). Minding the gap between positivism and hermeneutics in psychoanalytic research. *Journal of the American Psychoanalytic Association, 54*: 571–610.

May, R. M. (1976). Simple mathematical models with very complicated dynamics. *Nature, 261*: 459–467.

Moran, M. G. (1991). Chaos theory and psycho-analysis. *International Review of Psycho-analysis, 18*: 211–222.

CHAPTER ONE

The strange attractor

James Rose

T his chapter is an introduction to the concept of the strange attractor and its relevance to the study of the mind. As this concept is referred to repeatedly by the contributors to this book, though in varying ways, the editors felt that an introduction to this concept at this stage would be helpful for the reader. The idea of a strange attractor comes from the theory of complex non-linear systems. It refers to a pattern of cyclical dynamic motion towards which such a system tends when responding to external stimuli, which disturb its internally determined processes in some way. It comes from the observation that consistent patterns can be observed in the behaviour of iterative non-linear systems over a period of time, even though the system might appear, at any one moment, to be behaving randomly. They are seemingly "attracted" towards these patterns even if, within them, they might seem to become unpredictable. In psychoanalysis, it can be applied in understanding the patterns of internal representations and internal object relationships, or patterns of affect that can be observed in the transference and countertransference interaction.

Scientific investigation of a living system has involved identifying measureable variables descriptive of the system and observing how these variables interrelate in response to some external stimulus. Some (e.g., Davies, 1987) have thought that it is easier to start to think about the *strange* attractor by thinking about *simple* (or what are also known as point attractors) attractors in the mechanical, not the psychic, sense. Such attractors are commonly observed in linear systems, in which cause and effect can be related in a proportionate, reliable, and consistent fashion. An example is a pendulum, which is initially disturbed by displacement and which returns to a resting point as a result of friction in its pivot under the force of gravity. Plotted graphically, the oscillations will gradually dampen until the resting point is achieved. A pendulum is a simple one-dimensional system in which the energy of the initial disturbance is dissipated by friction and the force of gravity. It returns to a resting point and provided the pivot does not move, or the pendulum lengthen, the resting point will always be the same. Conceptually, this resting point can be seen as a *simple* attractor, which emerges when the response to disturbance is *linear*. That is, it is confined to oscillation around a fixed point in a single vertical dimension subject to the force of gravity, where the response to disturbance can be shown to be predictable according to a linear equation.

The problems of predicting the behaviour of complex dynamic systems has given rise to the notion of the non-linear system. The term refers to those systems whose behaviour is describable only by considering the interaction of the components within the system and between the system and the environment in which it is situated, and not simply by the linear summation of the system's functions, as in the case of the simple pendulum. As described by Craig Piers et al. (2007),

> a non-linear dynamic system is a system whose evolution is discontinuous, non-proportional, and unpredictable. Breaking it down: this means that, under certain conditions, non-linear systems change in sudden, abrupt, and discontinuous ways. Second, changes made in a component of a system do not necessarily have a corresponding proportional effect on the outcome. In other words, there is not always a clear and proportional link between cause and effect; small changes often have a profound effect. And third, even when armed with full knowledge of the current state of the system, we are unable to predict the future states of a non-linear system. In each of these ways, a non-linear system is different from a linear system, whose evolution can be plotted on a straight line and is continuous, proportional, and predictable. (p. 231)

We might say that a complex non-linear system responds to environmental influence in order to maintain itself. Its complexity enables it to do so with the flexibility essential for survival. A linear system responds in known and predictable ways to particular forces having an impact upon them but there is no implication that it is seeking to maintain its integrity.

Any living organism, which is interacting with its environment to maintain its survival, is, thus, by definition, a complex non-linear system. Such living organisms do not function solely as individuals, but are representative of a species and, therefore, part of a population of that species. This population is partly dependent on each individual member for functions that will maintain it: for example, reproduction. Over time, the size of a population will be determined, in any one year, by the food supply, the population's fertility and death rate and any other factor that affects fertility, such as the weather or disease. These factors may well interrelate. They represent inputs that determine an annual output: for example, rise or fall in population.

Over a period of years, the process of reproduction is an iterating one. Year on year, the actual size of a population depends on its size at the beginning of the year. It is affected by the impact of potentially random variables, varying year on year, which affect birth rate and survival. Conceivably, these variables can be combined into equations defining these complex systems

In considering the rise and fall of an animal population over time, certain conditions might prevail so that the species becomes extinct. However, while the population is in existence and maintaining itself, the exact number will not be annually predictable. Instead, it tends toward a range of values unless there is a catastrophic event: for example, an epidemic which kills many of the population. In normal circumstances, it may be found over time that annual population numbers are moving around unpredictably *within* this range of values. Annual population numbers will tend to this restricted range of values in the same way as our pendulum returned to a discernible point, but the single point of rest of the pendulum is replaced by this restricted range of values, which has come to be known as a *strange attractor*. This restricted range of values can be thought of as a space rather than as a point, as is the simple attractor. This space is not necessarily three-dimensional because it is determined by the number of variables needed to define the state of the complex system. It is

called strange because it was originally termed an attractor of fractional dimensions (or a fractal attractor). Living in a three-dimensional
world, we are used to think of dimensions as being unitary. The
concept of fractional dimensions is strange indeed. It is a concept
emerging from the study of potentially chaotic complex systems,
which can seem strange because they are unpredictable. An example
of the application of these ideas to the study of the rise and fall of
animal populations is given in Chapter Five.

What relevance has the concept of the strange attractor to thinking about the mind?

The mind can be thought as an epi-phenomenon of the central ner--
vous system but it is also a means of defining what it is about the
human being that experiences, as well as simply reacting. Of course,
it both experiences and reacts, but its capacity to experience makes it
hard to predict. It follows that any effort to predict such a system must
take experience into account. As a result, it seems beyond dispute that
the mind is unpredictable and, therefore, should be considered as a
complex system. Not only that, it has the property of self-reflection
and reacts to being studied by an external observer. This adds new
difficulties for any effort to predict its behaviour. In the past, this has
been thought to place limitations on what can be studied about the
mind. A consequent question is, how can we be objective about the
subjectivity of experience?

In essence, my argument is that the possibility of the observation
and identification of strange attractors in psychic reality arises out of
the continued iteration of the encounter between an analysand and his
psychoanalyst. There is no attempt yet to show how learning might
occur. However, if we postulate that all learning systems display
features common to iterative systems, that is, iterating intake, transformation of intake, and output feeding back into the system, then
understanding some features of these systems has a clear relevance for
psychoanalytic practice. My intention here is to offer some thoughts
on how our understanding of the workings of the psychoanalytic
learning system can be enhanced if we consider what has been found
about iterative systems, not just in the empirical sense, but also what
is to be expected about how *any such* system will function.

In the broadest of outline, we can say that the task of the psycho-analyst is to offer observations and interpretations on the ongoing process between the psychoanalyst and analysand in the light of the situation as it unfolds between them. In the light of these observations, the psychoanalyst and the analysand might be able to make links between how the analysand experiences the here-and-now, their past, and their future. These links will arise from the psychoanalyst's expe-rience, that is, her feelings and conscious reflections on these feelings. Through working in this way with the analysand, the defences devel-oped in his past life will become observable and, thereby, implicitly or explicitly, challenged. These defences will be manifest in the observ-able patterns of emotion in the psychoanalytic process.

Provided the psychoanalyst does not impose his own understand-ing on the process emerging between the psychoanalyst and the analysand, the emerging relationship between the two of them will be isomorphic with the object relationships in the analysand's psychic reality because the psychoanalyst remains, as far as possible, neutral. It will, thus, be capable of being both observed and experienced by both parties in the transference and the countertransference. We might infer that more frequent exposure to these patterns of experience made possible by more frequent sessions should make them more observable to both the analysand and the psychoanalyst.

This is the stuff of psychoanalytic learning and is never simply cognitive, but potentially saturated with affect. With this comes the possibility of change because the defences, created by the patient to deal with difficult experiences, are gradually revealed to be ineffec-tive. Nevertheless, there is no avoiding these experiences in the pro-cess of change. With this confrontation comes the threat of the possibility of chaos as the defences threaten to collapse and anxiety is aroused. Yet, the experience of the defences against these anxieties provide the impetus to change as these defences are revealed to be ineffective or, indeed, to be partly responsible for creating the anxi-eties against which they are supposed to defend.

The magnitude of Freud's achievement in his study of experience is reflected by the fact that he developed a method of observing the complexities of the mind: the creation of a setting within which con-sistencies and unconscious determinants of experience could be observed. From this, he developed a conceptual model of the struc-ture of the mind enabling the study of the relationship between a person's impulses, anxieties, and defences that contributed to an individual's conscious experience. By such means, he could take into account the differences between individuals in their conscious experience. This, coupled to the self-reflective capacity of the human subject, meant that an individual could get to know himself in a new way.

The main psychoanalytic technique used to investigate subjectivity is observation in a readily predictable setting. This opens it to an attack that the observed, being based on perception rather than measurement, will be subjective. Therefore, does this not lead to muddle between the observer and the observed? The development of thinking about countertransference seeks to deal with this potential muddle of the experience of observer and observed in the analysis of the relationship between analyst and analysand. Rigorously confining analysis to this relationship seeks to make it more objective because it is readily observable and available to both parties. Some, however, say that this runs the risk of impeding the process of free association and, therefore, limits both parties' perspectives.

The principal stimulus to the participants' experience of the psychoanalytic learning system is the iterating presence and absence of the analyst and analysand from one another. This creates changes in the interactive processes between the two and it is this that becomes the focus of observation. What commonly emerges are the analysand's characteristic ways of relating to those important to her as made manifest in her relationship to her analyst. These are referred to as the analysand's internal objects in her psychic reality. Thus, over time, the iterative quality of the psychoanalytic process enables the mapping of the analysand's psychic reality in the immediacy of the session and how it has developed in the course of her history.

Thus, learning occurs and, as it accumulates, it will become an additional input in so far as the analysand accepts and/or rejects what he is learning. Rejection, in part, will inevitably occur because certain defensive patterns of behaviour and affect have been developed to enable the individual to survive. Giving them up will threaten the individual with possibly succumbing to the very threats against which these defences were, or are in the process of being, created. For example, adolescents are difficult to treat psychoanalytically because intervention can be seen by the adolescent as threatening to undermine the development of his personality.

Observation of the analysand's psychic process can only be reliable when we allow a sufficient number of iterations—or sessions—so that we can identify the consistencies and, thus, the strange attractors which govern a person's psychic life. Hence, psychoanalytically, an analysand's strange attractors represent characteristic patterns in the relationships he has with his psychic internal objects. An example of a strange attractor is given by Graham Shulman in Chapter Five.

As these become observable, choices are presented to the analysand about how he wishes to manage these relationships. Resulting changes and their effects can then be reviewed and provide a new source of learning. These patterns are more than descriptions of relationship with others. They are descriptions of situations in the sense, perhaps a broader sense, of that described by Joseph (1985), see p. 47, below.

For an example of this description, when an analysand says that he does not know what to say, there can be a sense of something happening which is transmitted through the atmosphere or feeling of the session. Botella (2014) suggests that this reflects a time before words in the analysand's life or the characteristic atmosphere of his life that is so pervasive that it ceases to be considered in consciousness. An obvious implication is that the characteristic patterns of behaviour and experience cannot be established with any consistency by one observation or one consultation.

Second, we can observe how these strange attractors come to be formed and this may offer new means of intervening in this process of development. This could enable more effective defences against anxiety to be created. If these strange attractors are seen as reflecting situations providing a context for object relations, then a more complete description of an individual's psychic reality can be established. Further, if we can observe development in these terms, then we will be observing the development of an analysand's capacity to learn about himself.

Third, we must assume that psychic development can never be a smooth and gradual process. It will be characterised by discontinuities, which can be a source of considerable anxiety. Observing this might seem a departure from Bion's admonition to approach each session free from "memory and desire". However, it must be true that it is not only the analysand who is learning in the analytic situation, but the psychoanalyst as well.

Last, consideration of the psychoanalytic process as an iterating learning system offers new ways of thinking about how the psycho-analytic method of investigation works in the way it does. A specific example concerns why increasing frequency of meeting per week increases the potential for learning and thinking about how learning and resistance to that learning become manifest. Focusing on this aspect of the psychoanalytic situation has a number of implications for psychoanalytic technique.

One of these is that of having the focus of clinical attention as the situation as well as the immediate object relation. In recent years, there has been a controversy about the clinical importance of working in what has been called the "here and now" and eschewing attention to a patient's history. This position is, perhaps, derived from an assumption of a linear notion of time, which sees the passage of time as a line moving from the past to the present and on to the future. Supporters of the "here and now" position feel that it avoids the possibility of the discourse between analyst and analysand becoming an avoidance of the immediate affect between the two of them. On the other hand, an assumption of the non-linearity of time makes it possible to see how past, present, and future are all present in the "here and now". Seeing the existence of recurrent patterns of relationship between the two participants in a psychoanalysis, in all three tenses, makes it more possible to be in the heat of the situation and stand apart from it, thereby viewing the recurrent patterns. This means that the total situation cannot be seen as simply the immediate present in a concrete sense. The "here and now" will always involve the past and the future. Therefore, statements about the past and the future will always reflect the present. Such statements may reflect displacements from the intensity of the present—hence, defensive—but they may also reflect an analysand's self-reflective functioning and, thus, her learning. Only the process of the session will reveal their nature in this respect.

This book seeks to explore these implications in a manner that could be of help to practising psychoanalysts and psychoanalytic psychotherapists.

References

Botella, C. (2014). On remembering: the notion of memory without recollection. *International Journal of Psychoanalysis, 95*: 911–936.

Davies, P. (1987). *The Cosmic Blueprint*. London: Heinemann.
Joseph, B. (1985). Transference: the total situation. *International Journal of Psychoanalysis, 66*: 47–54.
Piers, C., Muller, J. P., & Brent, J. (Eds.) (2007). *Self-Organizing Complexity in Psychological Systems*. New York: Jason Aronson.

CHAPTER TWO

Experimental psychology and psychoanalysis: what we can learn from a century of misunderstanding*

Paul Whittle

This chapter is a personal and informal ethnography of the subcultures of psychoanalysis and experimental psychology. It is a case study in incommensurability, and was written out of frustration with the incomprehension that each side displays toward the other. The two disciplines shared many common origins, but each now views the other, by and large, with indifference or hostility. I sketch some reasons why their relationship generates discussions, such as those concerning the scientific status of psychoanalysis, that are like trains passing in the dark. I make some tentative suggestions as to why we may always need such different styles of psychology, and for what different goals, and personal and sociological reasons, we have developed them. I make even more tentative suggestions as to what, if anything, we should do about it.

Since it derives its structure and its liveliness from the occasion, it is being published as a record of the talk, with informal style and local

* This paper was first presented to the Zangwill Club of the Department of Experimental Psychology, Cambridge University, in April 1994. The paper was subsequently published in 2009, in *Neuropsychoanalysis*, 1: 243–245. It is republished here with the kind permission of Taylor & Francis Ltd.

allusions, rather than in more conventional journal-article format. Two subcultures. Second, it was an example of the subcultural differences I was talking about. Natural scientists like to talk with minimal notes, prompted by their visual aids, and often encourage interruptions from the audience. They believe they are reporting their interaction with nature, their words and diagrams being merely transparent media, and that their informal style testifies to their openness and honesty. In arts contexts or in psychoanalysis, these assumptions are thought naïve, and "talks" are generally read from finished scripts. As a boundary-hopping scientist, I often feel excluded by this style. I can't keep up, and I often want to interrupt and query the assumptions. I miss the more open interaction of a scientific seminar. Nevertheless, I found myself doing it. These different attitudes to language are a key to what is going on.

Credit

In 1897, W. H. R. Rivers (1864–1922) was appointed to the first post in experimental psychology at Cambridge. He was a doctor, a physiologist (his 1900 encyclopaedia article on vision was "the most accurate and careful account of the whole subject in the English language"), a founding father both of the department and of British social anthropology. What is less often remembered is that he was also a major contributor to the spread of psychoanalysis in Great Britain, in two books stemming from lectures given here and based on his experience as a psychiatrist with First World War soldiers.

Here he is writing in *The Lancet* in 1917:

> It is a wonderful turn of fate that just as Freud's theory of the unconscious and the method of psychoanalysis founded upon it should be so hotly discussed, there should have occurred events which have produced on an enormous scale just those conditions of paralysis and contracture, phobia and obsession, which the theory was especially designed to explain. . . . *There is hardly a case which this theory does not help us to understand – not a day of clinical experience in which Freud's theory may not be of direct practical use in diagnosis and treatment.* The terrifying dreams, the sudden gusts of depression or restlessness, the cases of altered personality amounting often to definite fugues, which

are among the most characteristic results of the present war, receive by far their most natural explanation as the result of war experience, which by some pathological process, often assisted later by conscious activity on the part of the patient, has been either suppressed or is in process of undergoing changes which will lead sooner or later to this result. (Rivers, 1916, pp. 164–166, emphasis added)

So, here we have another neurologist, probably a more careful and cautious scientist than Freud, reporting the same phenomena that Freud observed, but now of British soldiers not Viennese women, and agreeing with key components of Freud's explanation and treatment. I had read Rivers as an undergraduate, but forgot about him until reminded by an American feminist historian, Elaine Showalter, talking in the Department of History and Philosophy of Science. I think the roundabout route by which I relearnt the history of our department is also significant (Whittle, 1999).

One reason I start with Rivers is that he is so close to home. I could spend an hour telling you stories of other people whose lives link this department or Cambridge to psychoanalysis. In talking about psychoanalysis, we are talking about something deeply interwoven both as practice and thought in British intellectual culture. Particularly in this department, in spite of appearances. Here, it is a cultural unconscious.[1]

Introduction

My topic is the fault line running down the middle of psychology. On the one hand we have experimental psychology as practised and taught in virtually all academic departments of psychology; on the other hand we have psychoanalysis, the Freudian tradition and its offshoots, which is much more influential in the culture at large. I shall take for granted, though with some elaboration shortly, that both traditions are alive and well and creative and in their own terms successful, and that the gulf between them is enormous.

It would give my talk a good resounding start if I could say with conviction that this split down the middle of psychology is an intellectual scandal. But I am not entirely convinced that it is. I have a sneaking suspicion that it may be a political compromise that allows a division of labour in which both sides can get on with their work without too much disturbance. In the 1990s, working political compromises are coming to seem increasingly attractive, even when one sees clearly that they also have serious costs. In this case, there are two heavy and obvious human costs. The first is borne by students, who come to psychology hoping to learn about human nature, including their own, and find that the teaching institutions have been kidnapped by a particular style of thought.

This is so in many subjects, but what makes it galling, and, I think, unjust, for those psychology students who are not uncomplainingly socialised into the tradition offered them, is first that experimental psychology has such a monopoly in universities,[2] and second, that it is obvious that there is another way of thinking about ourselves which is also called "psychology", which is adopted by large numbers of intelligent people, which has just as impressive a history and literature as the tradition they are taught, and which would probably tell them more about human nature, particularly their own. As well as this cost to students, another personal cost is borne by those who later depend on the services of these same students, if they become psychologists. They have been educated in only one tradition, and their clients' needs may sometimes be better met by the other one. Many would argue, having in mind, for example, the American experience of the dominance of psychoanalysis in psychiatry over the 1940s and 1950s, that this applies also to the clients of those who are trained in that tradition.[3] That already gives ample justification for being concerned about the gulf. A further motive is intellectual. The people on both sides are talking about overlapping sets of difficult problems. It seems obvious to the point of banality that the perspective of each side must sometimes be helpful to the other, and it is easy to see many ways in which the perspectives of psychology and psychoanalysis complement one another.

Another way to put it is to argue, as many have, that the mixture of ideas with which Freud started, one foot in neurology and one in interpretation (or however you like to describe the other place), was a fruitful mixture, even if it contained confusions. It clearly did bear fruit. The obviousness of this combining-perspectives argument is what does make some outside observers see the split in psychology as an intellectual scandal.[4] Yet, by now, after a century of history, to most psychologists this argument seems naïve. It is naïve in the form I have so far put it. I have spent years crossing to and fro over the gulf, unable to commit myself wholeheartedly to science or arts, yet I rarely find myself able to take suitable gifts from one side to the other. In general, neither side wants what the other side has, and when they do, or I think they do, they are put off by the wrapping. But this is puzzling, to put it mildly. If both sides are thriving and creative and their problems at least overlap, how is it that their subject matter and/or their methods have led to such a continuing separation? Even if we don't want to build bridges, we should surely at least be curious about the geology of the intellectual landscape.[5]

A final reason is the extraordinary *fin-de-siècle* replay, with a cast of thousands, of exactly the dilemma on which the early Freud was impaled: are memories of what we now call "child sexual abuse", but which Freud more gently called "infantile seduction", genuine or fantasy? This makes it harder than even ten years ago for psychologists to see psychoanalysis as old hat. I could add that while cognitive psychologists' interventions in this furore may have a useful calming effect, they might well be more effective if they had not cut themselves off from half the relevant literature. That sketches the situation I want to talk about.[6]

I now become somewhat more specific, and start by elaborating what I said I take as given. I proceed partly by an informal ethnography and history of the two subcultures based on my experience of crossing to and fro. I hope this won't seem too self-centred. I like to think that it is a graspable and unpretentious level. I think it is also an important level, because science is culture, and an essential preliminary to any philosophical treatment, which I am not particularly competent at and which leave many audiences cold.

What I'm taking for granted

First, the continuing achievements and creativity of both sides. Both are strong and vital intellectual traditions. I mean this in a quite superficial sense, as an observation that could be made by a Martian looking at the two institutions, attending their meetings, reading their literature, listening to their discussions, seeing how much demand there is for their services, and so on. In case there are those in this audience who need reassuring about the current vitality of the psychoanalytic tradition, I will mention, rather at random, three manifestations of it. One, the renaissance of psychoanalytic thought in France over the past few decades, where it has become the vocabulary for articulating much psychological and social and political thought, with lasting repercussions in feminist and in literary theory throughout the Europeanised world. To anyone in the English or Modern Language faculties in this university, this goes without saying. It is a symptom of what I am talking about that this may not be so in experimental psychology. Two, the fact that postgraduate courses in psychoanalytic studies are springing up by the dozen in British universities. Three, even closer to home, there is the growth over the past fifteen years in Cambridge of a community of psychodynamically orientated psychotherapists, now numbering around a hundred. These are just three out of many examples I could point to of its vitality. Only in the USA, where psychoanalysis suffered the fate of being for a time an orthodoxy, is it frequently asserted that it is moribund. I need even less to argue for the vitality of psychology. Situated in the overlap of cognitive science, neuroscience, evolutionary biology, and the social sciences, it cannot help but partake of the ferment in all those areas (particularly the first two). This sort of vitality shows that a tradition is alive and well in what one might, since Foucault, think of as the domain of power–knowledge to indicate that it involves social and political components of practice as well as "knowledge". It does not mean that there are no major problems with either field; indeed, rather the opposite, since liveliness and problems often generate each other. So, both are working subcultures. Any of us could be in either of them, but for chances of temperament and biography. In either, we would find criteria for explanation and truth that there would be no more and no less reason to question than there ever is. That's a fundamental premise of this talk. It's where I stand. You can gloss it in anthropological terms, seeing cultures as the prime influence on both practice and knowledge, or in Wittgensteinian terms as forms of life or language games, or postmodernist terms as different discourses. It is an injunction to strongly respect and notice cultural boundaries, but not, as I take it, to cease looking for common human characteristics.[7]

I also take it for granted that both traditions work in a somewhat less relativistic sense. Experimental psychology is, in its better exemplars, cumulative, and strong enough to support various kinds of technology, which is the most straightforward criterion of a successful natural science. Psychoanalysis increases personal insight. In what sense this insight is "true", and how much it helps to solve the problems that people bring to therapy, are other, and difficult, questions, but that people in psychoanalysis have many convincing "aha" experiences about themselves I do not think is worth disputing. Further, psychoanalysis provides concepts that are widely found useful in talking about ourselves and our lives. I mean both in ordinary life and in special domains such as social or literary theory. In most cases, these concepts were borrowed from ordinary ("folk") psychology in the first place, but psychoanalysis has refined and deepened them.

The third thing I take for granted is the magnitude of the gulf between the two traditions. The size of this split within what outsiders regard as a single subject is without parallel in any other academic discipline. Neither side reads the literature of the other. On the whole, they don't try to: it does not seem interesting or relevant. If they do try, they find it almost impossible. To each side, the literature of the other seems profoundly misconceived. Everything seems wrong; the obscure motivations of the writers, their impenetrable jargon, what they take to be appropriate method, and their criteria for truth and relevance. These come together in a powerful gestalt, so that the literature has so strongly the wrong feel to it that it becomes unreadable. To many on each side it seems so obvious that the other is trapped within particular ideologies, institutions, political stances that they shrug their shoulders and do not attempt debate. It is a gap between different subcultures, encompassing different belief systems, practices, and institutions, vocabularies and styles of thought.[8] It is comparable to the gap between the religious and the irreligious, and, just as that gap is commonly felt not to be a profitable subject for discussion after adolescence, this gap, too, is accepted and ignored, and those who, like Hans Eysenck, persist in reminding us of it, are felt to be showing bad taste or some psychological peculiarity.[9]

Of course, there are exceptions. There are psychoanalysts like Bowlby who would be at home in a department of experimental psychology; there are experimental psychologists like Keith Oatley who are at home in psychoanalysis. There are even some who, with striking though surely ill-founded optimism, are announcing the merging of the two traditions (Erdelyi, 1985; Horowitz, 1989). In social and in clinical psychology you can find many who draw from both traditions, and you can find many ideas and practices, such as cognitive therapy, which are deeply indebted to psychoanalysis but do not advertise the fact. These exceptions all exist, but they usually turn out on closer inspection to be exceptions that prove the rule; for example, in the case of the people I've mentioned, you find they are disregarded or thought of as "unsound" by one or both sides. The overwhelming situation is one of separation.[10]

Water under the bridge

I should say something of the standard history and philosophy of the relationship. I think of this as "water under the bridge". Given my title, you might well expect it to be my main topic. But my perception of the situation is that both sides are stuck on these issues. I need to summarise them to stop you wondering about this and that, but they have become boring. This is both cause and effect of the gulf. To get things moving, we need to go up a level, to try to get an overview. Hence my cavalier treatment of these issues over which blood has been split, and over which passions can still be readily aroused. (So, the boringness is defensive?) It is not only water under the bridge, but also a minefield strewn with dead horses. The last thing I want to do on these topics is to flog dead horses.

Both traditions share an origin in Helmholtzian physiology, the tradition from which experimental psychology springs, and in which Freud was educated.[11] Early relations between the traditions were cordial. For example, William James was in the audience at Clark University, Massachussetts, in 1908, an occasion that Freud called the first public recognition of his work, and said to Ernest Jones afterwards that "the future of psychology belongs to your work" (Jones, 1955, p. 64). Psychology's cultural revolution towards behaviourism ended this harmony. Interest in psychoanalysis became, and has remained, a minority interest in psychology.[12] It was sustained, and still is, outside psychology, notably in anthropology and psychiatry. Attempts at "experimental verification" of psychoanalytic propositions. Overall conclusion equivocal (not negative). I come back to it shortly.

There are a few areas where there is more contact; for example, dream research in sleep labs. But again, early promise has somehow faded away. Why? One quite likely reason is that to progress, such work needs the intimate individual knowledge that psychoanalysis gives. Labov and Fanshel's (1977) study, *Therapeutic Discourse*, is another interesting example of interpretative psychology that found itself in that dilemma. But this demand for intimate knowledge breaks the conventional boundaries of laboratory research, and also becomes almost the same genre as psychoanalysis: individual interpretative studies with all their epistemological difficulties. Developmental psychology is an area that still includes Freud in textbooks, but unassimilated. Here again, the story is of occasional forays (like Piaget's psychoanalytic period).[13] There would seem to be plenty of scope for interpretative laboratory studies of children's play (like Klein, or Anna Freud, or Erikson), but it hasn't much happened yet.

Another community of psychologists that has much of the openness that I admire in some psychoanalysis, and that partly overlaps with "human sciences", is constituted by those who work in a broad evolutionary–biological and perhaps developmental, and sometimes cultural, framework (like Freud). These communities act as a leaven, but for some reason that I don't understand they remain only a leaven within psychology, rather than transforming its substance. The obvious inference is that psychology is only half-baked, as many have suspected.

"Outcome studies". Does psychotherapy "work"? This literature is founded on the hope that states of human misery, arising, for example, from unemployment, incest, homelessness, years of loneliness, spiritual despair at the violence and heartlessness of the world, can be seriously helped by a few sessions of scientifically structured intervention by somebody with psychology training. If psychoanalysis fails the test, then so much the better for psychoanalysis. I hope that clinical psychologist colleagues will permit me a little rhetorical exaggeration, but that is one valid critique of that literature (which I borrow from a clinical psychologist, David Smail (1987, 1993)). Another weakness of this literature as a critique of the truth of psychoanalysis is that there is no logical connection between knowing the truth about your life and leading it more successfully. They may even be inversely related, as Freud himself suspected.

There is a whole different approach to which my conscience occasionally recalls me. This is to work like that by Malan (1979) to extract a consensus body of "low-level observations such as all (psychodynamic) clinicians use". The defence mechanisms of repression and projection would be prime candidates. These are observed daily by all therapists. There are thousands of descriptions in the literature (and in Shakespeare and . . .; they are folk psychology) which could, if you wished, be assembled into a boring but surely overwhelmingly convincing body of public evidence. If experimental psychology has difficulty replicating them in the laboratory, then so much the worse for experimental psychology. There is no shortage of good reasons why this might be so.[14] They may require real emotions, genuinely part of someone's life, not feelings such as can be called up by a supposedly unpleasant word on a screen in a laboratory. To distinguish regression from mere forgetting may require knowing a lot about a person, knowledge of a kind that requires time and trust, and, therefore, a relationship of a kind not readily obtainable in a laboratory, and there is the rub. These are indeed "low-level" observations for psychoanalysis, but they are not so for psychology. Far from being a body of knowledge that transcends the difference in subcultures because it is so obviously grounded in our common humanity (as many clinicians feel) it may, in fact, be the topic about which most argument has raged. By now it is another dead horse. To see why requires changing the level of discussion, as I am trying to do.

I imagine clinicians saying this can't be right. These things are so humanly obvious. But it is right, while people stay in their subcultures. To get them out of it you have, for example, to take an experimental psychologist by the scruff of the neck and put him or her in a situation where they have to start seeing differently. This happens in individual therapy, or is happening to some in their encounter with the child abuse furore. To get a psychodynamic psychotherapist to start seeing the need for public, conventionally scientific evidence, you perhaps have to put their jobs under attack so they have to justify themselves and their practice to administrators. (I'm not sure about that; there are too many other ways out.) But in both cases it will not be just individual opinions that will change. They will start seeing all sorts of things differently. Their "eyes will be opened". This is the force of talking about subcultures. Beliefs, attitudes, behaviour, percepts, come in packages.

I mentioned "the standard philosophy" of the relation. I cannot discuss this properly; I am taking a different tack. I will just mention it. The part that is standard in psychology departments is the well-known

Popperian objection to psychoanalysis as unfalsifiable. It is both right and wrong.[15] It is another dead horse. The part that is standard elsewhere is the argument that is older than psychoanalysis, about the proper methods of natural and human sciences (*Natur-* and *Geisteswissenschaften*). Causes, reasons, agents, hermeneutics, Verstehen, etc. It helps in many ways, but it's not my approach just now. (For an accessible treatment, see Taylor (1971).) Some of you may be thinking something like, "He's already conceded to Popper with all his talk about arts and science and so on. He admits psychoanalysis is not scientific." But I don't want to come out and say that, for a variety of reasons. First, we no longer know what science is. Second, there are ways in which psychoanalysis is more scientific (by anybody's definition) than experimental psychology; for instance, in its openness to the reality and subtleties of experience. Third, the statement is so loaded that it's another dead horse: it has succumbed under its load. Fourth, I think psychoanalysis is probably vital to psychology, but that the real challenge is to develop new categories for thinking about it (as probably for other topics we are stuck on, like consciousness). I now go on to discuss why there is a gulf and what constitutes it: what are the contrasting aspects of the two subcultures that keep them apart?

What experimental psychology and psychoanalysis do

First, let me give a bald presentation of the different enterprises of experimental psychology and psychoanalysis (Table 1.1).

Table 1.1.   The differences between experimental psychology and psychoanalysis.

	Experimental psychology	Psychoanalysis (clinical work)
Aim	Public science	Individual therapy and enlightenment
Method	Observation and experiment	Personal relationship
	Impersonal and statistical	Interpretation and theory
Subject matter	General laws of behaviour and mental life (primarily rational)	Individuals (emphasising the irrational)
	Mental processes	Mental "contents"

This is a table of emphases; of course, you can find exceptions to each item. It points to resources for explaining much of the gap. Each item brings with it moral, political, and institutional dimensions which are not explicit in my table, but interrelate with every cell of it, and are dialectically related both to the enterprises and to their separation. How we treat, and so think about, ourselves and each other. Keywords: technology, science, medicine, welfare, control, power, hegemony, sociology of knowledge. Many of you may feel we could stop here. All right, they are very different enterprises. Of course there is a gulf, of course there are different cognitive styles, and so on. Why go on? Well, my enterprise is to persist nevertheless in trying to put perspectives together: an addiction to trying to see with the eyes of another culture. The moral imperative is "only connect" (E. M. Forster, *Howard's End*). Working in a department of experimental psychology and knowing many psychotherapists continually makes me feel this is quixotic. I gave reasons at the start for persevering, but we can now glimpse some of the reasons why we may not succeed. But the success of what? I wrote the last sentences back in the attitude that is natural to me of hoping for a single superordinate story that we might call psychology. But maybe connecting is possible, but not in that way. Maybe that is not how the pieces fit together. One persuasive attempt at fitting the pieces into a single story has been offered by Stephen Frosh (1987, 1989) in two recent books.

He argues that psychoanalysis has given us the best psychology of individual subjectivity that we have. Its enterprise (see Table 1.1) makes this likely. Experimental psychology shies away from subjectivity and particularly individual subjectivity, the contents of individual minds. But, most people ask, how could that possibly not be of the highest relevance to understanding human behaviour and experience? If Frosh is right, and I think he is to a considerable degree, this is a most obvious way in which psychoanalysis has something vital to offer to psychology. Frosh, in fact, pursues this in detail through different topics from artificial intelligence to gender differences, suggesting in each case important questions, ideas, and explanations that psychoanalysis raises but psychology does not. A strong reason for "minding the gap", which is the subtitle of one of his books. He offers the most straightforward and fully worked-out answer to the question of what psychoanalysis has to offer psychology.

However, although Frosh is admirable and unusual in bridging the gap, my guess is that most psychologists would not much like the suggestions he makes. A major reason is that they come wrapped in too much theory. To cope with that problem, we need to get back to the ethnographic comparison of the cultures, to try to see what this theory is doing and how psychologists could (perhaps) learn to love it, or, at any rate, to stomach it. The rest of this paper will be based on the assertion that the main tool or method in psychoanalysis is to fill gaps in self-narratives and self-awareness—the "talking cure", as Anna O, the first psychoanalytic patient, named it. That was its starting point and that is what it still does. We are aware of only fragments of ourselves (as experimental psychology also strongly holds). Many of the gaps can be convincingly filled by stories, using the psychoanalytic method. This is simply the common experience of people in therapy, that such stories can be convincing and sometimes helpful to them. They can be convincing also to others who know enough of the background. You can always ask for stronger criteria of truth, as psychologists or philosophers do. The questions are, "What for?" and "Are there any?"

This is the natural conception of psychoanalysis for our language- and text-centred era. To most analysts, however, it is superficial, because it ignores the structural changes in defences or personality that therapy aims at. Another radical qualification comes from thinking about the existential and moral dimensions of therapy. These are actually the heart of it. Therapy is not primarily talking about the patient and her life. Language is used more to show than to say (Heaton, 1968, 1972).[16] From this point of view, the descriptive psychology that the psychoanalytic literature is so full of is only a spin-off, not the main point at all, and may be even an escape from it. One answer to this comes shortly.

The different cognitive styles of the two sides

I want now to talk about the different cognitive styles of the two sides. I'm trying to give some feel for the experience of crossing to and fro between subcultures. Each side tends to be blind to the kinds of excellence admired by the other. This is important in maintaining the gap. I think the differences in style are an important part of it, and are not to be dismissed as "mere style". They embody cognitive habits that are crucial to the goals of the two subcultures. I start with a quote from Adam Phillips, a psychotherapist who also publishes as a literary scholar. It is from his engagingly titled book, *On Kissing, Tickling and Being Bored*.

> One of the dramas that these essays try to sustain—and that is present in every clinical encounter—is the antagonism between the already narrated examined life of developmental theory and the always potential life implied by the idea of the unconscious. The conflict between knowing what a life is and the sense that a life contains within it something that makes such knowing impossible is at the heart of Freud's enterprise. So in one kind of psychoanalytic writing the theorist will be telling us by virtue of his knowledge of development or the contents of the internal world what a life should be like, however tentatively this may be put. And in another kind of psychoanalytic writing—which in its most extreme and sometimes inspired form pretends to ape the idea of the unconscious—there is a different kind of conscious wish at work: rather than informing the reader, there is an attempt, to echo Emerson, to return the reader to his own thoughts whatever their majesty, to evoke by provocation. According to this way of doing it, thoroughness is not inciting. No amount of "evidence" or research will convince the unamused that a joke is funny. *And by the same token ambiguity, inconsistency, or sentences that make you wonder whether the writer really knows what he is talking about, are considered to be no bad thing.* I prefer—and write in these essays—this kind of psychoanalysis, but each is impossible without the other. Their complicity is traditionally underrated in psychoanalysis. (Phillips, 1993, p. xix; emphasis added)

First, note Phillips's style. Lovely subtle writing of a type unfamiliar and inappropriate in science. And he nicely describes, and admires, psychoanalytic writing of a more extreme kind. Lacan comes to mind, who took as his peers the Surrealist friends of his youth. Psychology comes out very differently that way from the way it does when you take medical textbooks as your model. Note the italicised passage. If you can't take that on board, you are not understanding how different psychoanalysis can be. Note also how he answers the problem I just raised, by pointing to the need for two kinds of language in psychoanalysis: descriptive and "inciting". This might also be our answer to the gap: the descriptive is scientific and the other something else. Unfortunately, the descriptive, for example Freudian or Kleinian developmental psychology, is doubtfully scientific in the judgement of most scientists, and still seems to function in psychoanalysis primarily as rhetoric, even though not of the "inciting" kind.

Understanding, in this subculture, often means to be able to discourse interestingly about something. To write a subtle net of language in which every sentence is compact with meaning sparks off free associations in several directions, and maintains an elusiveness and ambiguity that is true to life. Phillips exemplifies it. If understanding is to be able to speak evocatively about something, then this is understanding to the nth degree.

If understanding is to be able to "predict and control", then this is nothing. It offers no particular points of leverage, and such points are the *sine qua non* of technological action on something. But, of course, the experience of psychoanalysis is that it is precisely such discursive understanding, the ability to speak in evocative ways, that does offer leverage on ourselves. Indeed, Richard Rorty (1991) goes so far as to describe it as a "Baconian" instrument in the human context. Contrast the style of experimental psychology. Wittgenstein's famous dictum (1918) is a good start: "What can be said at all can be said clearly, and what we cannot talk about we must pass over in silence" (*Tractatus*, preface). You say it clearly. You do not use teasing words like inciting or whatever their majesty, which work, if they work at all, the scientist feels, in indirect ways, and only for particular sensibilities. But note this is all acculturation. The person who can appreciate Phillips instantly may not be able to stomach an experimental psychologist talking about the same thing. She may be so aware of the number of begged questions and so put off by the crudity of the categories ("Is it cognition or affect?" Of course, it is always both, this is human experience we are talking about) that she can't hear it.

Here is another description of the style of scientific thought, taken from Nietszche:

> It is the mark of a higher culture to value the little unpretentious truths which have been discovered by means of rigorous method more highly than the errors handed down by metaphysical ages and men, which blind us and make us happy. At first the former are regarded with scorn, as though the two things could not possibly be accorded equal rights: they stand there so modest, simple, sober, so apparently discouraging, while the latter are so fair, splendid, intoxicating,

perhaps indeed enrapturing. Yet that which has been obtained by laborious struggle, the certain, enduring and thus of significance for any further development of knowledge is nonetheless the higher; to adhere to it is manly and demonstrates courage, simplicity and abstemiousness. (Nietzsche, 1878, 1.3)

This catches beautifully, I think, the faith and cognitive asceticism of experimental psychology. The deliberate refusal or self-denial of understanding. Although psychoanalysis is also revolutionary in the type of understanding that it aims at, it doesn't at all have this asceticism. Rather the opposite. This kind of asceticism may be just what you need for experimental science, but just what you do not want if you are trying to fill gaps in a text or a life. For this interpretative synthetic enterprise, you need all the help you can get, all the concepts, all the associations, all the lateral thinking possible. Another obtrusive component of the cognitive style of psychoanalysis is its heavy use of theory.

The role of theory

The British are notoriously distrustful of theory. Newton was even, famously, distrustful of "hypotheses". Theory is continental. We think of it as Germanic, and heavy. We think of Hegel and Heidegger. Brits who get entangled in it, like Samuel Taylor Coleridge, or R. D. Laing, become incoherent substance abusers with marital problems. Psychoanalysis is full of theory. It has to be, because it is so distrustful of the surface. It could still choose to use the minimum necessary, but it does the opposite. It effervesces with theory, so infectiously that books of theory now bombard us from Paris, New Haven, Indiana, it sometimes seems from everywhere where there is a feminist, modern-language academic. This weight of theory is a major reason why experimental psychologists, who are the most deeply British–Empiricist culture that there is, cannot get on with psychoanalysis. How could they possibly? How could people whose habit of mind is to ask of every statement that might have empirical content whether (1) it is statistically significant, and (2), more interestingly, whether there might not be another, simpler explanation, possibly stomach these outpourings of prose, of sentence upon sentence of uncertain epistemological status? But stop a moment. This theory effervesces. It is not Germanic and heavy.[17] It makes jokes (albeit somewhat esoteric ones), it is laced with jouissance, with sexual ecstasy. Teresa Brennan (1993) writes in the introduction to her most recent book, *History after Lacan*, that "Feminist theory is the most innovative and truly living theory in today's academies". A scientist who looks into such books and who is involved in, say, the creative excitement of molecular biology or computational vision, may think she is simply off her head, but she is not.[18] What you can find there, I know from personal experience of both books and seminars, is a unity of heart and creative mind that is indeed extremely unusual, in universities or anywhere else, and is to be valued most highly. So, what is happening here? What is happening, in a word, is play. This is theory as creative play. Playful theory. It is a way of exploring the connections of diverse aspects of our lives and experience, juggling them this way and that to see if they could be made to fit differently, making new concepts so that we can grasp certain configurations as wholes, and use them as tacit units in further thought. Imagining societies with different child-rearing practices, after which men might not hate women so much. Imagining different ways in which our psyches may be constructed: perhaps one of them will mesh with our experience sufficiently to be a useful way to think of ourselves (since we don't know how our psyches are constructed). Now, of course, it is not labelled as fiction or play. That would risk malign influences from the ambivalence of our culture to those forms. It would discourage some readers and theorists from taking it seriously, weakening the commitment required to grapple with such difficult thought. It is better to leave its epistemological status genuinely uncertain in the minds of all concerned. But I think that, nevertheless, it can usefully be seen as play, a form of play to which we bring the same schizoid blend of willingness to identify and emotionally commit oneself, with the suspension of many ordinary commitments, that we bring to stage plays or film or fiction. Which, incidentally, even psychologists are sometimes willing to admit are both more serious and truer to life than psychology is.

A play space

This notion of a play space is relevant in so many ways to what I am talking about. Psychotherapy provides it. Psychoanalysis itself needs it. I recently heard Mary Jacobus, a distinguished feminist literary scholar, talking about Melanie Klein's lengthiest case history, concerning a child called Richard. Psychologists who try to read this don't know what to make of it. Klein deluges her young patient with interpretations, so that anything Richard says or does is as much a response to them as a reflection of his own state. What is observation, what is interpretation, what is suggestion? But, treated as a work of literature, it immediately revealed all sorts of new facets, including psychological insights to which otherwise I would have been blind. It was the right intellectual space into which to take it. When I'm lecturing on psychoanalysis, I annually complain that Freud's concepts are ignored; psychology has not developed them in the way it has developed those of Helmholtz, Pavlov, or James, for example. This year I realised that I was looking for them in the wrong place. In a recent seminar in Cambridge, Elaine Showalter took up the rhetorical question "Where have the hysterics gone?", and jokingly answered, "They have gone into discourse" (because of the amount of feminist writing, both theory and novels, on hysteria). Where have Freud's concepts gone? They have gone all over the place, into ethnography, the ethnology and sociology of the body and emotions (vital background for understanding hysteria), feminist theory, literary criticism, and, in due course, some of them will come home again to psychology changed and deepened and ready for us if we need them, or choose to attend to them. Psychology did not provide the right culture for them. This is not necessarily an indictment of psychology, which was doing its own thing, fighting its own battles, and the resulting environment was not hospitable to these memes.

You may ask, but doesn't all creative work need this? How is it particularly relevant to psychoanalysis? (1) It is a model of the heart of the process. Provides space for the person. The therapist as court jester. (2) It is more explicit in psychoanalysis (and is open to misinterpretation as claiming to be something else: scientific findings; the misconception I was trying to dispel). The play theory is published and public. Maybe in science we need to give more space to "speculations", as we call them. I have often felt we need to give more space to "understanding", and that is a form of theory. We pride ourselves on the discipline that experimental methods provide. But maybe we resort to them too quickly and should play more. Here is another quote from close to home:

Freud's strength [was] the most complete loyalty to facts as he observed them, an unshakable [belief] in his interpretation of the facts, a vast power of intuition or insight, and a great sweep of brooding imagination. In fact he raises in a most intriguing form the question of criteria by which a man is to be called a scientist. *It may be that all the great scientists are people who work as artists in a field which everybody considers to be scientific.* (Bartlett, 1955, p. 206, emphasis added)[19]

Why human nature may need a bipartite psychology

We are this creature that constructs itself in culture from ideas, memories, and so on, often from narratives, which seem fundamental to our thought in so many ways (think of dreams). We do this from birth, at first in a highly confused way that we don't know how to describe. Hence, the individual tangles of ideas in our heads that are what psychoanalysis works on. These are the prime source of personal meaning. That is to say, all meaning that controls our thought and behaviour. But they are full of gaps.

Pluralism

One of the hidden themes of this paper is the notion of truth. In scientific work, "truth" is usually a workable concept. If I'm asked, "is it true?" I have ways of finding out. In psychoanalysis, I no longer know what it means.

Psychologists have argued a great deal about the truth of psychoanalytic interpretations, and students often find them hard to swallow, argue for this or that other interpretation, and conclude that this vagueness damns the enterprise.[20] Both assume that there should be a single true interpretation in the same way that scientists aim for a single true explanation (at a given level). This is also why the existence of many schools of psychoanalysis is thought scandalous. But is not a better analogy the multiple interpretations that a poem or other text allows? They complement each other, and allow a multi-dimensional, or multi-perspective view of the object. This does not mean that "anything goes". You can still argue, even "rigorously", about how valid a particular interpretation is, and you can hope that the different perspectives in some sense converge, and do the intellectual work to show how they do or do not. Consider how easily you accept my two totally different metaphors for a certain body of work: "water under the bridge", and "a minefield strewn with dead horses". Two psychoanalytic interpretations for an item of behaviour or a dream might be equally different, but also both valid, that is to say, enlightening. This seems a good analogy if the subject matter of psychoanalysis is like a text with holes in it. The different interpretations of a text create a new one like coral growing on some nucleus. That is what life is like; it is forward going. Each new interpretation changes the person. Who can tell what the original coral was like? Does it matter? The interest is in what the new organisms brought. Their behaviour was only in minor respects determined by what they found. It depended also on their own nature and on the nutrients that happened to be flowing by and many other factors. A useful organic metaphor for mind? An ecological niche for memes. The best way to know it may always be to see what lives in it. And whatever lives in it changes it.

Two final quotes to help make such pluralism more attractive (perhaps). You can relate them either to the coexistence of two types of psychology or to the coexistence of alternative explanations within psychoanalysis. One quote from Nietzsche again: "Truth is a mobile army of metaphors". Another quote from one of the wonderful books that Don Cupitt, our local radical theologian, produces annually. Cupitt had in mind clearly contradictory interpretations of God. But his remarks are equally applicable to possibly converging interpretations of the psyche. The problem of power is acute in that domain too.

> "But that is a horrific position to maintain!" it will be declared. "You are saying you would rather keep the intellectual pleasure to be got from contemplating the endless clash of opposed views than discover one of them to be right. . . . You actually prefer pluralism and intellectual aestheticism to salvation by the Truth?" Yes indeed, because we are Westerners and not Muslims. My problem is—and perhaps it is yours too—that although I profess to love truth I could not actually endure a One-truth universe, because even as the angels ushered me into heaven I would still be nourishing the suspicion that it was all trumped-up, an illusion generated by power. I . . . would rather contemplate the conflict of two great truths and feel I had a choice between them, because that possibility of choice disperses power a

little . . . you are the same, probably, so it sounds as if we Westerners actually prefer and have chosen the nihilism that has engulfed us. We gave up Truth and sold our souls, all for freedom's sake. (Cupitt, 1990, p. 114)[21]

How psychology and psychoanalysis should cohabit: advice and problems

A psychology of individual subjectivity may always be as problematic as psychoanalysis. A century of history is enough to raise this as a possibility that we should seriously entertain. It is not popular in science to use history as part of our evidence, but maybe it should have some weight. You can't have any more certainty than in ordinary life. Epistemologically, psychoanalysis is folk psychology vastly developed (Gardner, 1993). By the same token, it is human understanding, and a lot of it. Something should also be said about personal temperaments and institutional constraints. Both are so important in maintaining the divide that the whole talk could be about them.

Personal temperaments: divergers, convergers (Hudson, 1966). Experimental psychology is dominated by convergent thinking, so, of course, psychologists have difficulty with a type of thought that is divergent in every respect, whose basic method, free association, is the paradigm of divergent thinking. But why is psychology so dominated by convergent thinking, even more so than other sciences? Is it really to the advantage of the subject? The divergent style that we see in theoretical physics is now found closer to us, in Artificial Intelligence. We often welcome it there, but why can't we nurture it ourselves? It is surely why experimental psychology is disappointingly less creative than one might hope, in the sense that it gets so many of its best ideas from outside (Shannon, von Neumann, Tinbergen, Chomsky, and so on) but has not yet generated ideas of comparable power for export.

Institutional constraints: no time to read; busyness; grant getting, not just for self but for department. These are currently of overwhelming importance in maintaining the cognitive styles and hence the gulf. This talk draws on years of random reading in fields not my own: professional suicide for a young scientist. Further, psychoanalytic training deeply involves and changes the whole person, not just his or her "knowledge". But to aim at that explicitly is counter to fundamental premises of university practice. Do all psychologists have to bother about psychoanalysis? Of course not.

What psychoanalysis offers psychology

This is a large topic on which I can make only one or two remarks here. I have already suggested that psychoanalysis tells us more about "human nature", in the colloquial meaning of that phrase, than experimental psychology does. Psychoanalysis speaks much more directly to us as human beings. Its teaching is, of course, only the current version of a long tradition, as Ellenberger's monumental history brings out so clearly (1970). The immediately preceding versions were the nineteenth century "unmasking psychologies" of Schopenhauer, Dostoevsky, Ibsen, and Nietzsche. I have already mentioned Frosh's work. There are many suggestions there that could help psychology towards its current goals. But psychoanalysis can also offer a critique of those goals, of the whole enterprise of scientific psychology, though that is another large topic that can only be mentioned here. For me, it offers an opening from psychology, in my teaching and reading, to all culture. One way of avoiding William James's complaint that "Psychology is a nasty little subject; everything one wants to know always lies outside it". What other topic would allow me to include in my lectures Hieronymus Bosch, Nietzsche, hypnotism, Northwest coast art, Shakespeare, Dostoevsky, the nature of love, sex, the relation of social structure to childrearing, etc., etc., all in one course and while plausibly maintaining that I'm still doing psychology? Of course, psychoanalysis is not the only route to all these things.[22] Ethnography is another obvious one. But psychoanalysis cannot be ignored. It offers another perspective. Just two words, but it is all there.

Notes

1. "It is history which is the true unconscious" (Emile Durkheim, cited as opening quote in Bourdieu's *Homo Academicus*, 1984).
2. A situation that is at present changing fast, but not in psychology departments.
3. Good examples for both sides are conditions like dyslexia or stammering, for which the choice of level-of-explanation that exists for all

behaviour is particularly open. Cognitive or neuropsychological analyses are relevant, but there will always be psychodynamics, too. In some cases, one level of understanding will be more appropriate, in others another.

4. It is an instance of a wider split that is often seen as scandalous. It is C. P. Snow's "Two cultures" split between arts and science. Psychology lies right on the fault line. The arts–science split was personally very real to Freud.

> I think there is a general enmity between artists and those engaged in the details of scientific work. We know that they possess in their art a master key to open with ease all female hearts, whereas we stand helpless at the strange design of the lock and have first to torment ourselves to discover a suitable key to it. (Letter from Freud to Martha Bernays, cited in Jones, 1953, p. 123)

5. I notice that fault line, gap, gulf, and chasm are the metaphors that come naturally to my mind. Not, for example, wall, river, or mountain range, which more commonly divide landscapes. What characterises the gulf, etc., is that there is no ground to stand on. They are not habitable zones, or places where you can stand, float, or sit even uncomfortably (as in "sit on the fence"). Yet we must and do "go up a level" to resolve differences between incompatible cognitive frames.

6. I outlined a topic, but not at all an argument. An alternative sketch I produced is a list of propositions that at least point to arguments: (a) psychologists need help with their/our reader's block about psychoanalysis; (b) psychoanalysis provides our best psychology of individual subjectivity; (c) we must come to terms with its incorrigible pluralism. At any scale, from interpretations to schools. We must learn to actually value this, not just tolerate it. Then we can pare down, perhaps, to only a few interpretations. But at present our scientists' obsession with the one truth, with either/or thinking, hampers us; (d) the same for its predilection for theory?; (e) on some plausible and common sense beliefs about human nature, the bipartite nature of psychology is to be expected and perhaps inescapable. This, too, suggests that we had better learn to love it. This talk is an essay, a discussion. I started with (e) as my`thesis, but that has shrunk in importance. A more open discussion came to seem appropriate. A single thesis draws the fire, where what I want to do is to leave a lot of issues more open than they usually are.

7. It does not mean that we are locked in our subcultures—think of them as overlapping sets—or that we cannot compare one with another, or critique one from another, or look for universal features of human nature. Clearly, we can, and this talk is an example of it. What it does mean is that you should respect the boundaries, be prepared for strong context dependence of what goes on within them, and for surprises ("culture shock") if you cross them. It is opposed to the fundamentalist attitude, Christian, Islamic, scientific, or whatever, that we either have or are approaching the one truth, but not to the hope that we may find truths in common. As an attitude to understanding other people, it needs to be complemented by its opposite, the faith that there is a common human nature, just as empathy needs to be complemented by detachment.

8. I once lived in a house to which a young anthropologist returned after his first extended experience of fieldwork. He had lived with a small Amazonian people for a year or two. On return to Cambridge everything felt wrong. The noisy streets, the cars, the density of people and their strange dress and gestures and motivations and attitudes. It seemed to go deep. He had come to be drawn to plump shiny girls who could make good beer. Most of all, his allotted task of writing a thesis had become abhorrent: to objectify these friends with whom he had lived, to whom he had probably entrusted his life. Now he had to write of their "artefacts" and their "kinship systems" in black and white on clean paper to be bound and put away in the University Library. After a week or two he had got over his culture shock, and was working again on his thesis, attracted once more to fair-haired waiflike girls. The gaps between biological and social sciences are wide enough to produce comparable phenomena. Byron J. Good, a medical anthropologist writes,

> Early in the course of our study of Harvard Medical School, we came increasingly to understand that learning medicine is not simply the incorporation of new cognitive knowledge, or even learning new approaches to problem-solving and new skills. It is a process of coming to inhabit a new world. I mean this not only in the obvious sense of coming to feel at home in the laboratories or the clinics and hospitals, but in a deeper, experience-near sense. At times when I left a tutorial in immunology or pathology to go to an anthropology seminar, I would feel that I had switched culture as dramatically as if I had suddenly been whisked from the small town in Iran where we carried out our research back into Harvard's William James Hall. (Good, 1994)

The gap between psychology and psychoanalysis is even wider. I personally used to undergo minor conversion experiences each time I crossed. Now I can do it several times in a day, which is in itself suspicious. (One is no longer "sound": may give off a hollow or cracked sound if tapped unawares.) I digress into these things because they are one indication of the personal roots of attitudes that we sometimes pretend are "merely academic". We are constructed and maintained by culture. When we are touching on these things, which is always, we are not wholly rational, because so much of this cultural underpinning is unconscious.

9. Here are some cannon shots fired from one set of trenches into the other: "The Freudian scheme is a tissue of unverified and often unverifiable hypotheses, all oversimplified" (McCulloch, 1965, p. 289).

"There will probably come a time when psychoanalysis is itself regarded as one of those curious aberrations of the mind to which man is periodically prone. Each age invents its own delusional systems" (Sutherland, 1976, p. 139). "Modern academic and experimental psychology is to a large extent a science dealing with alienated man, studied by alienating investigators with alienated and alienating methods" (Fromm, 1970, p. 69).

10. Organising the talk around the fault line is a particular choice. I could choose to ignore it, and so can you. I could talk from a community of my own choosing, containing, for example, Rivers, Merleau-Ponty, Bowlby, Shweder, Oadey, Gilligan, Frosh, Erdelyi. That is to say, people who are at home on both sides, and whom one can see as belonging to a "human sciences" community. There is no shortage of them, past or present, and a surprisingly large number have been connected with this department. This would be a fine brave strategy and I like it. But it would be like a Bosnian Serb marrying a Bosnian Muslim or Croat ten years ago. Entirely admirable, but understood by only a few in their community, and ignoring a deep-seated split.

11. More mischievously, one can see another common origin in alchemy and cabbalistic mysticism. Scientists don't think too much about this background, which was inextricably intertwined with science up to the time of Newton, but cynics readily see it still alive and well in, for example, medicine's faith in the attainability of magic substances to cure deep-seated human ills. Analysts, too, don't often refer to David Bakan's delightful book, *Sigmund Freud and the Jewish Mystical Tradition* (1985), which argues most persuasively for this as one root of Freud's emphases on sexuality and on word play.

12. There was actually a good deal of sympathetic interest in psycho-analytic ideas on the part of American behaviourists in the 1940s and 1950s (for example, Dollard and Miller, 1950), but this took the form of an attempt to transfer ideas, for example on the nature of psychological conflicts, into the different framework of animal behaviourism. An interesting enterprise, and not wholly unsuccessful, but with somewhat the air of a takeover bid, of showing that the "speculations" of analysts could be verified by the laborious methods of science. I contrast it with, for instance, James's *Varieties of Religious Experience* (1902), which shows the intellectual flexibility of an earlier generation of psychologists, their willingness to adapt their method to the demands of the subject matter.

13. Piaget was analysed by Sabina Spielrein. Thereon hangs a tale, which relates to my main themes in various ways. Spielrein first appears on the psychoanalytic stage as a psychotic patient in the Burgholzli hospital where C. G. Jung worked. He cured her, and they had a passionate affair. She was training as a doctor and became an analyst. Jung's marriage was threatened and he behaved badly, though he kept in contact with Spielrein. She was a creative thinker and influenced Freud as well as Jung. She possibly originated the idea of the death instinct. She analysed Piaget, and then returned to her native Soviet Union and worked with and influenced both Luria and Vygotsky. In 1941, the Nazis took all the Jews of Rostovon-Don, including Spielrein and her two children, to the synagogue and shot them. So, here we have this beautiful, talented, crazy young woman, weaving in and out of the lives of five of the most important psychologists of the century in the shadows of the Russian Revolution and the Holocaust, and possibly feeding them some of their best lines. And what do we do? We forget her. We forget her story and remain ignorant of her writings. We embalm the five Dead White Males in textbooks and inflict their embalmed thoughts on psychology students—and our own minds—severed from any connection with this vivid life that linked them. When we do remember her, the most salient feature is often Jung's bad behaviour, as though the really important thing was "the ethics of mental-health professionals". A depressing example of the way we sterilise and distort the living body of thought that we call "psychology". No wonder it is less creative than we would like (Appignanesi and Forrester (1992), give the best short account of Spielrein's story).

14. Not to mention the argument that some everyday knowledge is more fundamental than scientific, because scientific procedure depends tacitly on the former at every turn.

15. See Cosin, Freeman, and Freeman (1971), for one of the most effective rebuttals of the Popperian argument. Norman Freeman was a graduate student here, working on animal behaviour.

16. John Heaton was a student in this department under Bartlett. He became an ophthalmologist and wrote a unique account of the phenomenology of ocular disease. Later he became a psychotherapist, and founded, with R. D. Laing, the Philadelphia Association. He recently published the Wittgenstein volume of the *Beginners Guide* series of cartoon books for intellectuals. The Philadelphia Association still runs one of the most interesting psychotherapy training courses, attending to philosophy as well as to the psychoanalytic literature.

17. Neither is Germanic theory necessarily so. Denise Riley (1994) told us in a recent Cambridge alumnus magazine that when she was an undergraduate in the 1960s, copies of Hegel's *Phenomenology of the Spirit* used to circulate "like the latest hot novel".

18. I ignore her possibly specialist use of the word theory. In this section, I slip between a number of different kinds of theory. My intention was not to eulogise feminist theory (some of which I indeed admire, but some of which I do not), but to suggest a fruitful attitude to theory in general. I am acutely conscious here of the gaps between subcultures and the impossibility of finding the right tone. To anyone at home in the kinds of theory I am talking about, my attitude and style will seem patronising, primitive backwoods stuff. What wainscot is this man crawling out of? But to many of the scientists I know, most of this theory is either unreadable or beneath contempt or both.

19. Bartlett was the first professor of experimental psychology at Cambridge (1922–1952).

20. Forgetting William James's exhortation to psychologists to allow space for "the vague".

21. This is from a chapter entitled "A theory of God", which contains an appendix on Parallel Distributed Processing! Perhaps we are in a time when subcultures are converging rapidly. MIT can now offer a course on Heideggerian Artificial Intelligence.

22. I am often astonished, when I talk on this topic, by the need that some listeners have to classify me as a believer or not in psychoanalysis. I am not sure that I am a believer in anything. The kind of psychoanalysis I admire, for example, that of Winnicott or Marion Milner or Bion, is so heterodox that many would not at first recognise it as psychoanalysis. Psychoanalysis maintained as an orthodoxy—and it is strongly so maintained by some and some institutes—is as repellent as any fundamentalism. What is it about psychoanalysis that makes it necessary to say this?

References

Appignanesi, L., & Forrester, J. (1992). *Freud's Women*. New York: Basic Books.

Bakan, D. (1985). *Sigmund Freud and the Jewish Mystical Tradition*. London: Free Association Books, 1990.

Bartlett, F. C. (1955). Fifty years of psychology. *Occupational Psychology, 29*: 203–216.

Bourdieu, P. (1984). *Homo Academicus*. Cambridge: Polity Press.

Brennan, T. (1993). *History after Lacan*. London: Routledge.

Cosin, B. R., Freeman, C. F., & Freeman, N. H. (1982). Critical empiricism criticized: the case of Freud. In: R. Wollheim & J. Hopkins (Eds.), *Philosophical Essays on Freud* (pp. 32–59). Cambridge: Cambridge University Press.

Cupitt, D. (1990). *Creation Out of Nothing*. London: SCM Press.

Dollard, J., & Miller, N. E. (1950). *Personality and Psychotherapy*. New York: McGraw-Hill.

Ellenberger, H. F. (1970). *The Discovery of the Unconscious*. London: Allen Lane.

Erdelyi, M. H. (1985). *Psychoanalysis: Freud's Cognitive Psychology*. San Francisco, CA: W. H. Freeman.

Fromm, E. (1970). *The Crisis of Psychoanalysis: Essays on Freud, Marx and Social Psychology*. Harmondsworth: Penguin.

Frosh, S. (1987). *The Politics of Psychoanalysis: An Introduction to Freudian and Post-Freudian Theory*. London: Macmillan.

Frosh, S. (1989). *Psychoanalysis and Psychology: Minding the Gap*. London: Macmillan.

Gardner, S. (1993). *Irrationality and the Philosophy of Psychoanalysis*. Cambridge: Cambridge University Press.

Good, B. J. (1994). *Medicine, Rationality and Experience*. Cambridge: Cambridge University Press.

Heaton, J. M. (1968). Theoretical practice—the place of theory in psychotherapy. In: N. Bolton (Ed.), *Philosophical Problems in Psychology* (pp. 176–199). London: Methuen, 1979.

Heaton, J. M. (1972). Symposium on saying and showing in Heidegger and Wittgenstein. *Journal of the British Society of Phenomenology, 3*: 42–65.

Horowitz, M. J. (1989). *Introduction to Psychodynamics: A New Synthesis*. London: Routledge.

Hudson, L. (1966). *Contrary Imaginations*. Harmondsworth: Penguin.

James, W. (1902). *The Varieties of Religious Experience*. New York: Longmans, Green.

Jones, E. (1953). *Sigmund Freud: Life and Work*, Vol. 1. London: Hogarth Press.

Jones, E. (1955). *Sigmund Freud: Life and Work*, Vol. 2. London: Hogarth Press.

Labov, W., & Fanshel, D. (1977). *Therapeutic Discourse*. New York: Academic Press.

Malan, D. H. (1979). *Individual Psychotherapy and the Science of Psychodynamics*. Boston, MA: Butterworths.

McCulloch, W. S. (1965). *Embodiments of Mind*. Cambridge, MA: MIT Press.

Nietzsche, F. (1878). *Human, All Too Human*. Cambridge: Cambridge University Press, 1986.

Phillips, A. (1993). *On Kissing, Tickling and Being Bored: Psychoanalytic Essays on the Unexamined Life*. London: Faber and Faber.

Riley, D. (1994). My time at Cambridge. *Cam, Lent: 39*.

Rivers, W. H. R. (1916). *Instinct and the Unconscious*. Cambridge, UK: Cambridge University Press, 1920.

Rorty, R. (1991). Freud and moral reflection. In: *Essays on Heidegger and Others* (pp. 143–163). Cambridge: Cambridge University Press.

Smail, D. (1987). *Taking Care*. London: HarperCollins.

Smail, D. (1993). *The Origins of Unhappiness*. New York: HarperCollins.

Sutherland, N. S. (1976). *Breakdown* (2nd edn). London: Weidenfeld & Nicolson, 1988.

Taylor, C. (1971). Interpretation and the sciences of man. In: *Philosophical Papers*, Vol. 2 (pp. 15–87). Cambridge: Cambridge University Press.

Whittle, P. (1999). W. H. R. Rivers and the early history of psychology at Cambridge. In: A. Saito (Ed.), *Bartlett, Culture and Cognition* (pp. 21–35). London: Routledge.

Wittgenstein, L. (1918). *Tractatus Logico-Philosophicus* (Revised English translation, 1961). London: Routledge.

CHAPTER THREE

Chaos theory and psychoanalysis: the fluidic nature of the mind*

George Moran

F or many disciplines, the focus of study is a system that sometimes behaves predictably and, with a change in certain conditions, behaves in a complex or apparently random manner. In
meteorology, fluid dynamics, and ecology, scientists have constructed models of their respective systems, attempting to capture the
complex nature and behaviour seen in real life. Until the last ten or
fifteen years, such models consisted of numerous equations which
had to be "summed" in order to account for the variety possible in a
real world system (this was true when trying to model even the
simplest physical systems). Experimental observations that deviated
from the models were considered artifactitious, or the deviations were
resolved by the *addition* of more components or equations. Mathematical approaches to modelling have for a number of years examined
systems that work on themselves over time, that "flow". This
approach drops the previous notion of tag-on equations to encompass

* First published in 1999 in *International Review of Psycho-Analysis*, 18: 211–221.
Presented in a slightly different form to the Denver Institute for Psychoanalysis on
29 April 1988, and to the Denver Psychoanalytic Society, 20 February 1990. Copyright
© Institute of Psycho-Analysis, London, 1991. Reproduced with kind permission of
Wiley Ltd.

supposedly variant behaviour, and shows that complex behaviour can be determined by simple equations of a special class, called non-linear differential equations (May, 1976). Many systems that are so modelled work on themselves, or "flow": the old "output" becomes the new "input". This process of flow suggests images of fluids, and indeed it is in the discipline of fluid dynamics that much of the pioneering work has occurred. Such fluidic systems characterised by this kind of feedback are prone to exhibit "chaotic" behaviour over time: behaviour that is *apparently* random, disorganised, and without order. The science of these new models is in fact called "Chaos". The choice of the name is unfortunate, because there is little that is truly lawless, destructive, or totally disorderly about the field or its subjects of study. Indeed, the new models allow a clearer appreciation of qualitative and *quantitative* characteristics of complex systems never before possible.

This paper has several aims.

First, there has been no previous attempt to apply the principles of Chaos to a psychoanalytic model of the mind. Therefore, I will show how the mind might be viewed as a dynamic system, and how it shares characteristics of other systems that have been studied and fruitfully elucidated by Chaos theory. I do this by giving an outline of the main characteristics of the kinds of systems in question (non-linear systems). I will then show how psychoanalytic models of the mind resemble models of non-linear systems. I used original technical papers as the resources in formulating my concepts, but the chief thrust of this paper is the demonstration of a *formal* resemblance between the physical, mathematical models mentioned and the psychoanalytic models of the mind. Hurdles to the evolution of a specific methodology for psychoanalysis will be discussed. The references provide citations for those interested in pursuing the background for my work.

Second, I apply chaos theory to specific psychoanalytic phenomena. The applications are not to be taken as finished work; at this stage of my endeavour, closure would be stifling. The purpose of this second part of my paper is rather to indicate my present areas of interest, and also to stimulate further exploratory work by others. I examine some common clinical phenomena, such as dreams, and also subjects on a more abstract level, such as the mechanism of action of psychoanalysis.

The paper ends with a brief comment on the position and status of psychoanalysis among the other sciences.

Characteristics of non-linear systems

Non-linear systems are those whose behaviour is describable only by considering the *interaction* of the components *within* the system, and not simply by the *addition* of the system's qualities. The system's true nature can be understood or apprehended only by taking those inter-actions into account. That is, the summation of the components of a *single non-linear system* and its characteristics is less than or qualita-tively different from what one sees when the system is viewed as a whole. Many systems, previously assessed as "simple" are, through the perspective of Chaos, now understood to possess complex and strange behaviour. The pendulum is an example (Tritton, 1986). Equa-tions that account for behaviour of the pendulum through the mere summation of certain values (each of which represents a known char-acteristic of pendulum behaviour) will not be adequate when trying to describe the pendulum's potential for complex behaviour. According to old models, such behaviour would be seen as unrelated to the true, determined nature of the pendulum's activity. When different equations are formulated that take into consideration the *interactions* between a single system's different characteristics, a more accurate picture emerges. Mathematical models can then be constructed that better approximate the nature and potential range of the pendulum's behaviour. Movement that was previously considered accidental, or the result of random external influences, can be under-stood as determined.

As one uses such a constructed model to study the nature of a system, it becomes clear that the starting point for observation is crucial. The "path" taken by the system, and the resulting end point, change markedly when any starting parameter (such as the tempera-ture or velocity in a hydrodynamic system) is varied only slightly. This characteristic is called *sensitivity to initial conditions*.

Although non-linear systems may have arenas in which there is exactly repetitive or "periodic" behaviour, they virtually always have the capacity for *nonperiodic* behaviour as well. There may be globally recognisable patterns in the activity observed, but there is always focal behaviour with no apparent repetition. This capacity for complex and only near-repetitive activity is exclusive to non-linear system models.

In some multidimensional models of these systems, graphic display reveals shapes of great complexity. When magnified, the complex shapes recur, with infinite, idiosyncratic detail filling what appeared to be a very small space. Like Russian toy dolls, each ornate shape reveals another when closely examined. From the field of fluid dynamics comes a common example. When looking at the sculpted bottom of a creek bed through clear water, one sees a familiar pattern: regular, smooth, curved furrows. The entire pattern may be only inches across. From an airplane[*sic*] window one can see the same pattern, this time in the clouds below the viewer. Sculpted by forces millions of times more powerful and millions of times greater in their spatial dimensions than those at work in the creek bed, the pattern is similar: regular, curved furrows. Such self-similarity of stable, recognisable, even idiosyncratic forms and shapes, recognisable and similar at different scales of examination or magnification is called *scaling*.

The models constructed with the characteristics mentioned in the foregoing material allow a more inclusive exploration of *transitional states*. In hydrodynamics (from which the paradigm arises), scientists study the transition from laminar to turbulent flow. Examples from other disciplines include the transitions from conductor to superconductor and nonmagnet to magnet (Gleick, 1987). The onset of transition states and the nature of their substructure are described by Chaos *par excellence* for a large class of non-linear systems. In a system undergoing a transition of state, there is dissipation of energy in one form to a less usable form (for example, through the action of friction, kinetic energy is transformed into heat) (Hofstadter, 1981). Certain fundamental and universal principles about the states and about the principles guiding the dissipation for many physical systems have been clarified by chaos theory.

The next step in my exploration is to compare the characteristics of the chaos theory of non-linear systems with the model of the mind central to most psychoanalytic thinking, in order to determine whether there are sufficient correspondences between the two to warrant applications of chaos theory to clinical mental phenomena. What follows is a comparison of *forms* of non-linear systems models and the psychoanalytic model.

The interaction of various mental features is taken for granted in most psychoanalytic models, and is given formal importance in the structural model. From a phenomenologic standpoint, the psychoanalyst takes this view of the mind (as interacting with itself, or intraacting) into account when he considers, for example, the interdependence of the patient's affect, verbal associations, and sensations of physical posture on the couch (and this would be only three of many potential variables). These three variables, and, of course, many more, must be considered not only additively, but as to *how they relate to each other*, in order to understand the nature of the psychoanalytic process at any moment. The model of the mind that demonstrates some characteristics of linearity is the topographic: increasing unconscious pressure shapes the nature of observed clinical behaviour and productions. That is, a *summation* of the unconscious pressures on the patient's psyche that are striving for conscious expression might be considered one attribute of mental life at any time. From another perspective within the topographic model, mental activity might be seen as related in a linear fashion to any mental content's distance from consciousness. But the reductionism in such conceptualisations, even within the topographic model, is evident. It seems reasonable to conclude that any psychoanalytic model would encompass the concept of non-linearity.

The next attribute of non-linear systems, *"sensitivity to initial conditions"*, finds a home in the psychoanalytic concept of psychic determinism and in the importance of an individual's developmental history. Analysts see the individual's current mental life and behaviour as powerfully affected and determined by past experiences.

The existence of *nonperiodicity* in mental life is suggested in the complexity and variety of any individual's experience. There is little chance of exact replication by the psyche. Even the repetition of externally identical comments, actions, or thoughts could not be truly exact, because of the intervening slight accretions of historical meaning occurring with the passage of time and the accrual of experience. However, the *period* (or time span of a potential cycle of repetition) of an individual's mental life may be obscured by the events of life that act as perturbations "external" to mental life. Also, the total time required for repetition may theoretically exceed an individual's life span, and thus preclude documentation.

Although exact repetition is impossible, recurrence of patterns in mental life is a widely accepted phenomenon in psychoanalysis. On any level of examination, one can see a "signature" of the patient's characteristic mental activity: within the case history (at what might be called the lowest level of magnification), within the patient's productions in any single session, within a single dream, or even contained in a single slip (the greatest enlargement), one can make out a recognisable part of the patient's own particular, idiosyncratic pattern of mental life. Such patterning is *scaling* of mental phenomena.

Transitional states also have a place in psychoanalytic models of the mind, and can be conceptualised in several frames of reference. For example, transitions of state occur when the *effects* of insight have made an impact. The patient does not display these effects in an incremental movement from one kind of behaviour to another on a continuous spectrum. As analysts, we experience the patient as *being different* at those times of change. That is, there seems to be a qualitative shift in the patient's state. In addition, when the therapy is going less well, at times of an apparent "negative therapeutic reaction", one might describe the patient's state as having changed in what appears to be an abrupt manner. More familiar transition states (but located within different levels of abstraction) might be the changes involved in ego state, or self- or other representations. The point to note here is the thoroughness of the qualitative change, as experienced by the patient, the analyst, or both. Given adequately timed and sufficiently specific external perturbations, a chaotic system is capable of a number of states of relatively stable behaviour. In mathematical terms, chaotic systems may possess numerous *solutions*.

We may thus conclude that the mind, as modelled by psychoanalytic metapsychologies, intra-acts, displays sensitivity to beginning conditions, is likely to be nonperiodic, demonstrates scaling, and can be observed to make transitions between states. Since these are also the qualities of systems in other disciplines that have been fruitfully modelled using non-linear differential equations, it seems likely that there may be mental phenomena that can be productively modelled within psychoanalysis by applications of the tools of Chaos.

In order to explore further the possible applications of non-linear dynamics to the mind, I will now discuss in some detail the aspects of Chaos that have already been shown to be universal to dynamic systems in a wide variety of disciplines.

The discovery of these certain universal characteristics was achieved on purely mathematical models. No one yet knew how to model a physical system based on empirical data observed in "the field". In those early experiments, often conducted on computers, one-dimensional systems were studied, and the findings were startling. The scientists were able to predict with great accuracy the regions of system activity in which chaotic (turbulent) behaviour would appear. The rate of progression toward turbulence could also be predicted.

For adequate graphic representation of a system, each essential characteristic of that system's activity must be allocated a dimension. One-dimensional systems (graphed by plotting the output of the system against its output at the next time interval) can hardly be expected to model even a simple system in the physical world, much less something as complex as the mind. However, let us consider these low-dimensional models for the time being, for purposes of demonstration. To graph a turbulent stream, one might want to use (at least) two dimensions: temperature and velocity, for example. One might use only one dimension, but the resulting graphic portrayal might sacrifice a sense of genuineness about the nature of the system. In any case, one selects the essential dimensions, then plots them against each other as data is collected during the system's observed activity.

The tracing that is produced turns out to be a trajectory of a point moving through space (called phase space). The tracing represents every important characteristic and displays its activity *in relation to* every other important characteristic. Although experimentally unachievable in "the field", infinite time can be approximated by computer modelling. Graphic displays of such models give the scientist a new look at these systems: dimensions change with time and system activity. As a result of forces that dissipate the energy of the system, some dimensions contract, even drop out. Others enlarge, or increase. For example, with decreasing temperature in the hypothetical system above, velocity of the fluid movement may decrease; the graphic representation would show this dimension (velocity) contracting and deforming the shaping of the trajectory accordingly "inward". Temperature would also decrease, shrinking its dimensionality, and further deform the shape of the tracing "inward". The resulting graph of the system at asymptotic time would show the deformations worked by falling temperature on the dimension of velocity.

In this sample case, friction acted as a dissipative force. If the system were not driven in some way, and friction were either turned up or allowed to remain constant, the system would eventually grind to a halt, and velocity would be zero. As a consequence of the zero value the system would lose a dimension and, in this example, become one-dimensional (represented only by its temperature). The final graph would look like a thermometer: the entire nature of the system and its subsequent history could be shown through a single numerical representation: the temperature. If no further heat were introduced into our experiment, the whole system would be shown on the graph in phase space slanting towards a point: that single temperature reading. At that time, the point would have "attracted" all of the activity of the system, it would be a "point attractor" (Figure 1).

If we were to explore the possible applications of these models to the mind, we would be forced to consider more complex situations. What about graphs of driven dissipative systems of higher dimensions? Rather than a *point* encompassing an entire system, at asymptotic time, a spaghetti-like *shape* of bends and curves would represent the system's nature (see Figures 2 and 3); if all dimensions could be shown, the shape would contain all the information about the system and its history. There would be few if any points or lines of trajectory far from the "shape", because of its attractive "pull" on the graphic display of the system's activity. Blank areas of phase space would thus portray activity of which the system was incapable. The attractive

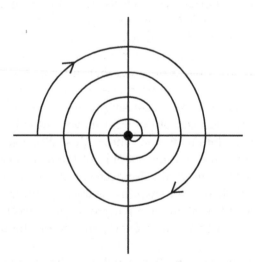

Figure 1.   A point attractor (after Brotman).

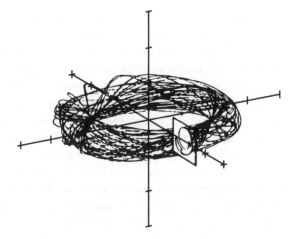

Figure 2.   A strange attractor (after Brotman).

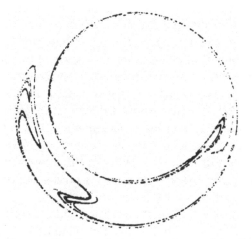

Figure 3.   Cross section through a strange attractor (after Brotman).

"force" operating to shape and deform the trajectory in such a multi-dimensional graph is called a "strange attractor". Strange, because of its complexity and the ability to induc e the phenomenon of "sensitivity to initial conditions". As a result of the activity of the strange attractor, minute differences in beginning conditions are channelled into widely divergent results at asymptotic time (Feigenbaum 1980).

Using appropriate differential equations, certain universal characteristics of many physical systems can be elucidated. Irrespective of the discipline, dynamic systems display similar behaviour that can be shown to be *quantitatively identical*. The first evidence for this universality came through experiments that were totally mathematical—not derived from experimental observation of physical systems "in the field". Still, the important similarity revealed itself: *no matter what was being modelled*, as long as the system being observed worked on itself over and over again, certain universal behaviours, as shown by numbers called Feigenbaum constants, revealed themselves. (The mathematical process that models the flow of a system over time is called iteration.) In a series of important later developments, experiments with some "particularly messy models of actual physical systems that exhibit turbulence" demonstrated that such systems were guided by the Feigenbaum constants (Hofstadter, 1981). Feigenbaum's universalities had been found to be applicable to actual, multi-dimensional physical systems.

The constants discovered by Feigenbaum can be used to predict the onset of turbulence in a dynamic system (or the particular quality that is analogous to turbulence). These numbers help to determine the rate of development of changes in state, such as the development of turbulence in the fluid dynamics paradigm (Feigenbaum, 1978, 1979). In other disciplines, the state change is usually a transition of a kind other than smooth flow to turbulent flow: non-magnetised to magnetised, for example, or conductor to superconductor. In the systems modelled by these equations, forces are at work that mould the state changes. It is by virtue of the activity of these forces that dimensionality contracts. And the strange attractor guides the contraction (and any expansions) that occur (Hofstadter, 1981).

Friction acts as a force that dissipates and affects the distribution of the energy of the smooth flow in a turbulent hydrodynamic system, thereby producing turbulence when the friction is great enough. When working with the mathematical models, the parameter in the equation that represents the degree of friction (or its analogue in another paradigm) can be "tuned" to represent a change in friction (May, 1976); when tuned high enough, turbulence begins, and is manifest in the equation's output: values begin jumping all over the graph (at first glance, a pictorial analogue of Chaos, but at asymptotic time the picture of the strange attractor emerges). Thus, the output of the mathematical model matches the behaviour of the actual physical system. Feigenbaum saw that the occurrence of turbulent behaviour approached at a predictable rate as he "tuned up" the parameter that designated friction or its analogue. That predictable rate of approach has been found to apply to the models of *all* non-linear dynamical systems thus far studied.

Franceschini and Tebaldi (1979) studied systems much more complicated than those described above: the models required five differential equations for accurate representation of the physical system. The investigators demonstrated the existence of typical strange attractors in their complex model. A team of an American and two Swiss investigators then proved that in multidimensional driven dissipative systems, at asymptotic time, all dimensions but *one* drop out, and the resulting behaviour is that of a one-dimensional system (Collet et al., 1981). What these experiments suggest is that as long as one has correctly characterised the system, the right "physics" can be obtained from some very crude models (Cvitanovic, 1984; Wolf, 1983). The key point here is that dissipative systems shrink in phase-space volume at infinite time. That is, dimensions tend to contract at infinite time, and simpler models then apply.

No study of behaviour, no analysis has permitted a complete examination of any person. Only total, lifelong study could exclude or confirm periodic behaviour. Lack of periodicity in human behaviour, while a common sense inference, is theoretically impossible to prove (Lorenz, 1963). But the chances of the mind's being a nonrepeating and non-linear system, if not acceptable as given, seem overwhelming. I have shown that the psychoanalytic model includes these features and others that are common to those models guided by non-linear differential equations of actual physical processes. The formal correspondences might then extend to the concept of the strange attractor and to the Feigenbaum constants.

In every other discipline where strange attractors operate, there is no referent for the attractor itself. That is, there is no clearly elaborated thing (or even conceptual analogue) for which the attractor stands. I believe that psychoanalysis has such a referent for strange attractor: the fixed collection of the patient's unconscious fantasies, his unconscious story (or collection of stories) about himself. Through the mode of the strange attractor, the unconscious fantasies, *though themselves very simple underlying structures*, become manifest in complex, multidimensional behaviour. From a psychoanalytic viewpoint, the *teleological* significance of the strange attractor's function would be the individual's enhanced ability to defend himself against awareness of that same unconscious set of fantasies. That is, the more disguised or complexly *rendered* is the fantasy set, the less likely is the patient's conscious recognition of those fantasies (and, hence, of the accompanying potentially unpleasant affects). Observable behaviour remains focally unpredictable, but globally predictable because it is all the while being "attracted", at asymptotic time, toward the core simplicity of the unconscious fantasy set. Put another way, no matter how diverse the behaviour may appear, it will, upon psychoanalytic observation, reveal the influence of *relatively* simple and finite unconscious fantasies.

The complexity of any attractor confers a certain stability on its long term behaviour. At asymptotic time, the attractor is the entire history of forces that drive or dissipate the system. Given any but catastrophic perturbations, the long-term behaviour of the system will settle back into the global pattern forged by the attractor. In a sense, the more complex the attractor, the more sophisticated the potential response of the system to perturbations. A simple attractor guides a system in a rigid, unsophisticated manner, and is subject to profound disturbances by simple external forces. (Remember the point attractor—the final temperature—in the simple system described earlier. Its capacity as an attractor would be limited by the stability of the system's thermal environment. The activity of the system thus protrayed would be driven by any events that could affect temperature. Since that attractor is one-dimensional, only that one dimension need be affected to totally drive or disrupt the system. Any number of factors could change the temperature, rendering the point no longer functional, over time, as an attractor.) The mental manifestation of a simple, nearly periodic attractor (such as an extremely limited set of unconscious fantasies) might be a severe character disorder, where variety and sophistication of available behaviour are critically limited in the face of perturbing events (external happenings or internal forces). An extreme example might be paranoid personality (here seen controlled by a very simple, and rididly applied set of unconscious fantasies): every event, internal or external, is experienced in only one way—as a threat or potential threat to the individual. Consequently, the range of adaptive responses would be quite limited.

This leads to some thoughts about the possible mechanism of action of psychoanalysis. Seen within chaos theory, the therapy may act as an extended series of well-timed perturbations which serve gradually to disrupt the strange attractor of the patient's fantasy–behaviour coupling in the direction of increased complexity. One might see the patient as coming to analysis with a (relatively) simple, nearly periodic strange attractor that is easily disrupted. Behaviour is predictable in certain dimensions; that is, it is maladaptive (and adaptive) in a relatively predictable manner, with a similar pattern over time. Through the well-timed and well-dosed perturbations (interpretations of defences, for example), the strange attractor acquires complexity. Analysis would be seen as tuning the attractor to a higher grade of structural intricacy. The shape of the strange attractor changes; especially, its dimensionality increases. As a consequence, behaviour (fantasy material, thought, cognitive patterns) becomes less rigidly determined (less periodic). More of any one phase space is visited by the trajectories of the system. That is, more behaviour is possible as dimensionality of experience increases. Of course, other ways of increasing the complexity of the attractor may be posited, and could include modelling, internalisation of certain ego functions of the analyst, and a variety of learning experiences outside of analysis (and one could doubtless offer others).

What is the mechanism of transition from a state of relative simplicity to a state of relative complexity of the strange attractor? In more familiar terminology, what is the mechanism of the transition from a state of low (or no) insight, to one of insight? Or, what is the mechanism of change? One mechanism for the route of change might be through the route of phase transitions. States of turbulence or near-turbulence would bring about manifest complexity of behaviour and an increase in (some) dimensions.

How might one understand the tuning variable called "friction" in the hydrodynamics paradigm, as it relates to the psychoanalytic model? One could see this variable as the point of intervention of the analyst. A conceptual analogue might be clinical "intensity", or analytic work that is "experience-near". The greater the clinical intensity, the higher the "friction" variable. Alterations in the variable perturb the patient's strange attractor, and change quasi-periodic activity into more complex, (potentially) more adaptive activity (Ruelle, 1980).

In early development, the intensity of the child–parent interaction might affect or set this tuning variable. As development proceeds, the sophistication of the attractor increases, and the child's adaptive abilities become more wide-ranging. A good parent is aware of the timeliness of his or her interventions and interactions, given the age and state of the child. Age-appropriate parenting would keep the tuning parameter within tolerable limits, and maintain a developmentally appropriate fit with the complexity and stability of the child's strange attractor. Sophistication of the phase space trajectories (representing behaviour or some other, specific mental activity) gradually increases with maturation. Interactions that are inappropriate in timing and intensity cause variations in the tuning variable that produce erratic or destructive mental activity, as seen in traumatic or overstimulated states. In this context, the "turbulent" or "chaotic" mental phenomena produced in these states are clearly maladaptive or destructive, as opposed to the creatively adaptive turbulence of an emerging state of insight. One could account for such variation in the potential clinical consequences of turbulence as due to the application of the perturbation within separate dimensions, or perhaps by tuning the "friction" variable to different points.

The Feigenbaum constants order the rate of emergence of turbulence in the hydrodynamic paradigm; what role do they have in the understanding of the onset of turbulent mental states? The constants are a theorist's blessing and an experimenter's curse (Cvitanovic, 1984). In this paper, my efforts have been aimed at theory, restricted from experimentation by what is perhaps the inevitable lag of methodology behind theory. However, even in the mathematical domain, theorists find the Feigenbaum constants much more friendly than do physical experimenters. The constants appear in even very brief examinations of a system's behaviour, bolstering the theorist's arguments. Experiments are cursed by mathematical quicksand: each iteration (or experimental run) requires an algebraic increase in the measuring accuracy required to document the Feigenbaum rates of convergence. Thus, even with strictly defined conditions, and very few dimensions, limited experimental resolution makes it currently impossible to observe more than a few steps in any real-world experiment. There are certain legitimate mathematical finesses (Holden, 1983) that might be used should a methodology evolve for psychoanalytic experiments within the domain of Chaos. And, as mentioned before, features inherent in non-linear system models might make low-dimensional approximations useful to the psychoanalytic scientist and clinician. Thus, there is the possibility that low-dimensional models may be useful to model the mind *when the system is viewed over asymptotic time.*

Chaos theory may help address one of the classic problems of psychoanalytic research: the need to collect massive amounts of data over a great deal of time. Because of the phenomenon of scaling, in which critical patterns become evident with a small fragment of a system's behaviour (or phase space), sufficient scrutiny of representative behaviour may yield basic and typical structures of the system. One key here is "representative behaviour". That is, if the starting conditions of any one experimental run are close enough to those typically seen in the system's activity (the patient's mental activity), the shape of the attractor will soon be evident (Ruelle, 1980). This premise is incorporated in Dahl's strategy for psychoanalytic research (see below).

Chaos theory may provide a new way to understand and incorporate recent neurophysiologic research on dreams (McCarley et al., 1981) without the gutting of psychoanalytic theory that such authors advocate. From some experimenters in neurophysiology come suggestions that brain activity during REM sleep is essentially random, with dream interpretation by the patient and analyst being a purely *ad hoc* activity. That is, the formal characteristics of dreams have no meaning *per se*; their idiosyncratic character (nonsensical, broken in time, existence of absurdities) only supports the "truly" random and purposeless character of dream manufacture (Hobson, 1985).

Chaos theory offers a different perspective. The strange attractor of a neurosis can be seen not only as the determining force for mental activity, but as a characteristic (for the patient) limit of random activity (Gleick, 1987). In this way, the experience (and meaning of the experience) resulting from what indeed may be random pontine neuronal firings would be limited by the strange attractor, whose experiential features these firings would then randomly "illuminate", much as an erratic electronic television gun might allow the display of only part of the determined broadcast picture. The strange attractor lays out the limits of dream meaning that can be activated by the neurologic events, just as the attractor does with experiences of waking life.

Many other tantalising questions arise: if the mind is a driven dissipative system, what is the most likely candidate for the driver(s)?

For the dissipator(s)? Might we see the therapeutic action of psycho-analysis as the interaction between the strange attractors of the analyst and the patient? Does Chaos tell us anything about the functioning of the *brain*, in addition to that of the mind?

In addition, there are technical issues of methodologic importance. In the experimental situation, what are to be the dimensions used to describe mental phenomena? What methodology will allow the quantification of mental activity within the designated dimensions?

One might criticise this paper for an apparent use of mind–body isomorphism: locating cause at one conceptual level and consequence at another, or mixing the languages of psychological and non-psychological disciplines. But I am not reducing mental events to brain events, and I am not suggesting an identity of cause for these two different kinds of phenomena. In this paper I make a comparison between mental phenomena and fluid systems on a *formal* level in the hopes of expanding our understanding of complex mental processes. Using non-psychological models to enrich and enhance the accuracy of psychological models is not the same thing as mixing levels of causality, such as attributing a physiological cause to a specific mental event. Chaos may indeed accurately describe brain functioning, and some aspects of non-linear brain functioning may impinge on mental phenomena. But I leave the exploration of that interface for another time. The phenomena I have sought to explore through non-linear dynamic principles are *mental* phenomena.

Some psychoanalytic writers suggest that there is no room for scientific inquiry within the psychoanalytic domain (Schafer, 1976). I obviously disagree. To paraphrase Ricoeur: the psychoanalytic situation "forces the activity of the mind to pass through the defile of words" (Ricoeur, 1977). Teller and Dahl, referring to the "words" of Ricoeur, describe the psychoanalytic research task in a way that may suggest to the reader, now familiar with some of the concepts of Chaos, the presence and importance of non-linear systems:

> If one takes these words, the patient's words, seriously, if one records them and transcribes them, if one searches and re-searches them, one is rewarded with the discovery of patterns and structures that are indeed there to be found, that are not merely invented or arbitrarily imposed on unwilling data. It is these words that we take to be the data of psychoanalysis. The scientific challenge is to show how to

represent (literally, re-present) these words to reveal the structures embodied in them and to establish their relation to accepted psychoanalytic facts. (Teller & Dahl, 1986, p. 765)

The ultimate proof of the usefulness of chaos theory in psychoanalysis will depend upon answers to the foregoing methodological questions. However, I feel there is merit in pursuing what I believe to be formal and theoretical correspondences between Chaos and psychoanalysis at this time. By expanding our understanding of possible relationships between the two, we build new bridges for communication of theory and methodology between ourselves and other scientists.

Many critics of psychoanalysis have attacked the field for its "unscientific" stance, its reliance on individual case reports, and lack of replicable outcome studies. I feel that the conceptualisation of the mind as a system organised by the principles of Chaos has the potential to add a new dimension for the explorations of researchers. Psychoanalysis is a science, a science with complex beings and activities as its concerns. Chaos could provide a more useful model for psychoanalytic methodology than do models derived from nineteenth century linear scientific thinking. Non-linear dynamics gives an approach more tailored to the nature of psychoanalysis itself: a science of non-linear events and organisms, dynamical in their interrelationships, whose development and continuation are sensitive to initial conditions, and whose inner structures are non-periodic and demonstrate scaling and self-similarity on close inspection.

Stephen Jay Gould has written eloquently about the criticism of evolution as a science. Much of what he says about evolution applies equally well to psychoanalysis.

The problem lies with our simplistic and stereotyped view of science as a monolithic phenomenon based on regularity, repetition, and the ability to predict the future. Sciences that deal with objects less complex and less historically bound than life may follow this formula. Hydrogen and oxygen, mixed in a certain way, make water today, made water billions of years ago, and presumably will make water for a long time to come. Same water, same chemical composition. No indication of time, no constraints imposed by a history of previous change.

Organisms, on the other hand, are directed and limited by their past. They must remain imperfect in their form and function, and to that extent unpredictable since they are not optimal machines. We cannot know their future with certainty, if only because a myriad of quirky functional shifts lie within the capacity of any feature, however well adapted to a present role. The science of complex historical objects is a different, not a lesser, enterprise. It seeks to explain the past, not predict the future. (Gould, 1983, p. 64)

Summary

Advances within the new science of Chaos have enabled scientists in several disparate disciplines to deepen their understanding of complex systems and to quantify certain phenomena called state transitions. These transitions occur where the nature of the system changes markedly, for example, when a fluid passes from smooth to turbulent flow. Non-linear systems (those that are modelled best by Chaos) are described in this paper and compared with psychoanalytic models of the mind. Some psychoanalytic phenomena are examined in the light of the principles of Chaos. The author asserts that there are sufficient correspondences between operative models in those disciplines that have benefited from the use of principles of Chaos and psychoanalytic models of the mind to warrant theoretical and experimental efforts in the use of those principles. Such efforts could enhance our understanding of the mind and may suggest a new methodology for psychoanalytic research.

References

Collet, P., Eckmann, J.-P., & Koch, H. (1981). Period doubling bifurcations for families of maps on R^n. *Journal of Statistical Physics*, 25(1): 1–14.
Cvitanovic, P. (Ed.) (1984). *Universality in Chaos*. Bristol: Adam Hilger.
Feigenbaum, M. J. (1978). Quantitative universality for a class of non-linear transformations. *Journal of Statistical Physics*, 19: 669–706.
Feigenbaum, M. J. (1979). The universal metric properties of non-linear transformations *Journal of Statistical Physics*, 21: 25–52.
Feigenbaum, M. J. (1980). Universal behavior in non-linear systems. *Los Alamos Science*, (Summer): 4–27.
Franceschini, V., & Tebaldi, C. (1979). Sequence of infinite bifurcations and turbulence in a five-mode truncation of the Navier–Stokes equations. *Journal of Statistical Physics*, 21: 707–726.

Gleick, J. (1987). *Chaos*. New York: Viking.

Gould, S. J. (1983). Quick lives and quirky changes. In: *Hen's Teeth and Horse's Toes* (pp. 56–65). New York: Norton.

Hobson, J. A. (1985). An agenda for a new psychiatry. *Bulln New Psychiatry Sem, 1*: 2–22.

Hofstadter, D. R. (1981). Metamagical themas; strange attractors: mathematical patterns delicately poised between order and chaos *Scientific American, 245*(5): 22–43.

Holden, A. V. (1983). Chaos in complicated systems. *Nature, 305*: 183.

Lorenz, E. N. (1963). Deterministic nonperiodic flow. *Journal of Atmospheric Science, 20*: 130–141.

May, R. M. (1976). Simple mathematical models with very complicated dynamics. *Nature, 261*: 459–467.

McCarley, R. R. W., Hobson, J. A., & Hoffman, E. (1981). REM sleep, dreams, and the activation-synthesis hypothesis. *American Journal of Psychiatry, 138*: 904–912.

Ricoeur, P. (1977). The question of proof in Freud's psychoanalytic writings. *Journal of the American Psychoanalytic Association, 25*: 835–871.

Ruelle, D. (1980). Strange attractors. *Mathematical Intelligencer, 2*: 126–137.

Schafer, R. (1976). *A New Language for Psychoanalysis*. New Haven, CT: Yale University Press.

Teller, V., & Dahl, H. (1986). The microstructure of free association. *Journal of the American Psychoanalytic Association, 34*: 763–798.

Tritton, D. (1986). Chaos in the swing of a pendulum. *New Scientist, 24*: 37–40.

Wolf, A. (1983). Simplicity and universality in the transition to chaos. *Nature, 305*: 182–183.

CHAPTER FOUR

Chaotic possibilities: toward a new model of development*

Robert M. Galatzer-Levy

M ost psychoanalytic models of development and change assume an orderly, sequential and predetermined unfolding of psychological functions and structures. Interferences with orderly unfolding challenge the individual and may lead to pathology. These models derive from a worldview associated with the descriptions of change through linear differential equations, which predict a smooth, orderly world. The study of complex systems and their associated non-linear dynamics predicts a very different kind of world: a world with abrupt changes, discontinuities, idiosyncratic developmental lines, and disproportions between causes and effects. The worldview of non-linear dynamics suggests new possibilities for the psychoanalytic model of change and development, and invites confrontation with the adequacy of many widely accepted models. These new possibilities include discontinuous, sudden and qualitative shifts not only in manifest behavior but also in in-depth psychological functioning.

---

* First published in 2004 in *International Journal of Psychoanalysis*, 85: 419–441. Reproduced with kind permission of Wiley Ltd.

Concepts of development rank second only to clinical experience in shaping analytic theory and practice. Despite its diversity, most analytic thought about development follows a pattern Freud borrowed from late 19th-century embryology in which preset steps smoothly unfold to yield a mature organism. Pathology can often be described as the result of derailments in normal developmental sequences. Most analytic debates about development focus on which of several sequential models is most useful in conceptualising normal and disturbed development.

Developmental ideas, acknowledged or not, pervade analytic theory and practice (Fonagy & Target, 2003). In the past many analysts worked as though paths of development were well-established facts and could be used with confidence in thinking about clinical work. Some analysts still maintain this attitude. However, with the appearance of competing developmental theories and the general lessening of theoretical–technical rigidity, this attitude has shifted. In their clinical work most contemporary analysts try to remain flexible, examining how well various developmental concepts apply to particular patients. Even so, we continue to listen to what patients say using specific developmental theories and general concepts of development. Some of these concepts have become so much part of analytic thinking that they are not even the focus of question. By introducing ideas of non-linear dynamic into the study of development in psychoanalysis I hope to enlarge the range of pictures available to clinicians and raise awareness of implicit conceptualisation as we try to understand clinical material.

The basic psychoanalytic model, the assumption of developmental sequences, may be questioned. The study of non-linear dynamics, popularly known as chaos theory and the theory of complex systems, suggest alternatives to the sequential model of development. This paper explores some of these possibilities and their significance for analytic thought and practice. To do this I first explore conceptualisations of development commonly used in psychoanalysis. I then describe some ideas from non-linear dynamics relevant to thinking about development. While describing each of these ideas I try to give examples of how the concept is relevant to a psychoanalytic understanding of development. Throughout this paper I use very brief clinical examples, not as evidence of the theory and certainly not to provide a full analytic understanding of the material but rather to

point the analyst/reader toward the type of clinical issues that can be
illuminated by non-linear dynamics.

The idea of development in psychoanalysis

Freud's discovery that the origins of neurosis lie in early childhood
experience, combined with his long-standing interest in embryology,
led him to explore psychological development. Analysts clarified
developmental models. However, starting with Freud they recognised
that the many factors operating on and within the child, combined
with the difficulty of assessing these factors, severely limited the
application of developmental concepts to individuals. Clinicians
commonly use developmental models as heuristic guides in understanding analysands. Many analysts are convinced that development
almost always follows specified outlines—psychopathology and therapeutic progress can be described by reference to the individual's
developmental status. Contemporary clinicians are less likely than
earlier analysts to try to force the stories of individual lives to the
template of developmental theory. Still, despite variations in its use,
the underlying model was unquestioned until recently. In this section
I briefly review how development has been seen in psychoanalysis.

Freud's vision of the relationship between development, psychopathology and treatment is founded in the idea that psychopathology
results from development gone awry. Specific failures of development
result in specific pathology, in the same way that specific embryonic
damage results (or at least was believed to result) in specific lesions in
the mature organism (Sulloway, 1979). To truly cure, treatment must
undo the effects of failed development, preferably creating a situation
closely approximating undisturbed development. Freud (1905d,
1908b, 1909b, 1914c, 1916–1917, 1923b, 1926d, 1940a), Abraham (1924),
and Reich (1949, 1975) pioneered descriptions of the impact of developmental problems, building a magnificently inclusive description of
personal distress and character based on developmental variations.

Later psychoanalytic theorists elaborated these ideas. They often
focused on aspects of development not included by other theorists.
Some argued that the early analysts were mistaken in their descriptions of development. Yet, the underlying strategy remained similar to
Freud's. Analysts described normal sequences of development, their

variations and the consequence of these variations for later psychological life. Klein (1923, 1928, 1935, 1937, 1945, 1957, 1969), Winnicott (1945–1958, 1953, 1958, 1960a, 1962, 1963a,b, 1965), Mahler (1952, 1958, 1968, 1971, 1972; Mahler et al., 1975), Kohut (1966, 1971, 1977), Gedo and Goldberg (1973) and Lichtenberg (1975. 1979, 1983), to mention but a few, followed this strategy.

Among major psychoanalytic thinkers, Anna Freud (1965) uniquely suggested that the fact of development, rather than its particulars, deserves a central place in analytic thinking. The concept of developmental lines arose from the observation that the concordant development of id, ego and superego, so beautifully outlined in Abraham's work, fit poorly with observations of children. Anna Freud also argued that the interaction of developmental lines is as important as the individual lines themselves. Clinical experience taught her that correlating children's development with age-typical norms failed to provide clear pictures of normal and disturbed childhoods. Instead she underlined that the failure of developmental progress is the central feature of childhood psychopathology. When development progresses, she said, even if it deviates from a norm, the child has engaged the major psychological task of childhood. When development does not progress, the child is disturbed, even though symptoms and other indicia of pathology are absent. Anna Freud concurred with earlier theorists that psychological development moved toward a final goal, referred to in the "drive to the completion of development".

Anna Freud's student, Erik Erikson (1958, 1963, 1964, 1968, 1978, 1982, 1984), enlarged the study of development in another direction. Freud's depiction of development was unappealing in that development is described as essentially complete (but for some modification at puberty) with the resolution of the Oedipus complex. Jung (1953, 1954) challenged this idea and was the first to describe development as ordinarily lifelong. Within Freudian psychoanalysis, Peter Blos, Sr. (1941, 1962, 1967, 1968) and Anna Freud (1958), among others, suggested that adolescence was a period of further development. But even these writers, consistent with their picture of development as moving toward completion, held that psychological and physical development shared an end point in late adolescence. Erikson posited that development continues across the life course. Two currently popular psychoanalytic ideas about life-course development are associated with the idea of a lifelong process of separation–individuation (Panel, 1973a,b; Schafer, 1973, 1976; Henderson, 1980; Rangell, 1989) and ideas of the self as transformed across life (Galatzer-Levy & Cohler, 1990, 1993).

Reviewing these psychoanalytic concepts of development we note that, except for Anna Freud's model, these can be encompassed as variations on Abraham's (1924) developmental chart, which correlates developmental phases. Analysts as diverse as Erikson (1963) and Gedo and Goldberg (1973) summarise their conceptualisations using such charts. In all these models development is described as occurring in an orderly series of steps roughly tied to the person's age. Satisfactory progress in each step is necessary for the full engagement in the next step. Psychoanalytic developmental theories share this feature with a wide range of developmental theories from other traditions (Case, 1992).

Many psychoanalytic controversies centre on which of these models, so similar in the sense of positing an orderly sequential unfolding of psychological function, is most satisfactory. Klein vs Anna Freud, Kohut vs ego-psychology, and ego-psychology vs id-psychology are each controversies about which of these sequential tables the analyst should use. A central question of analytic technique might be formulated as: given a developmental model, how is the patient to be moved from a less adaptive, more immature position on its chart, to a more adaptive, more mature position?

Experiences in teaching, writing about and explaining human development show how useful the idea of orderly sequential development can be. These models organise and make sense of vast and disparate data; they clarify communication; they are among our most powerful tools for understanding the psychological world. Only the concepts of conflict, unconscious psychological process and the self come close to being as useful in describing psychological life. The sequential developmental paradigm is so powerful that it appears natural and inescapable to many of us.

However, the seeming naturalness of conceptualising development as an orderly sequence may derive from its familiarity. This familiarity results in part because the psychoanalytic developmental paradigm rests on earlier and pervasive ideas about development. Reviewing how these ideas entered psychoanalysis helps clarify why they appear so natural. Freud directly borrowed the idea that psychological development is sequential from his study of embryology (Sulloway, 1979).

For Freud the pertinent general findings were as follows:

1. Embryological development is ordered and complex. How the embryo builds to its final organisation may not be obvious, but each step in the developmental sequence is part of an orderly process.
2. Wilhelm Roux showed that specific lesions of the embryo consistently produce specific later developmental changes and pathology. Because of the complexity of embryonic development, the impact of a particular lesion can only be understood as it affects the overall embryonic development.
3. Using Haeckel's principle that ontogeny recapitulates phylogeny, and equating social with biological evolution, Freud posited that less socially and psychologically evolved communities would manifest similar features to the immature members of more evolved societies.

Only the last of these three major ideas has dropped from current psychoanalytic thinking. In addition to the embarrassment it caused, it was empirically found to be false, as was Haeckel's original notion (Gould, 1977).

As it turns out, the experimental data from which Roux made his generalisation was not as strong as his writings suggested (Needham, 1959) and the link between lesion and outcome is not as strong as Freud believed. In addition, the apparent rigid unfolding of development apparent in early embryologic studies is now understood to be far less clear and far more contingent on the embryo's environment than was believed until recently (Dusheck, 2002).

In addition to its great utility, Freud's basic model has survived partly because it has had no significant competitor and partly because, as a result of their own analyses, most analysts are convinced about the impact of early experience on later development. This experience-based conviction is easily confused with the much more comprehensive notions of sequential development on which Freud and later psychoanalytic investigators' work rests.

Problems with the standard psychoanalytic
model of development

Because the assumption that development occurs in an orderly sequence is so powerful, it has neither been widely questioned nor has data supporting its broad assumptions been widely doubted. Almost from the beginning Freud recognised that limitations in our knowledge of individual lives and the complexity of the processes of development made prediction impractical in psychoanalysis. In a brilliant paper, which presages some of the ideas of non-linear dynamics, Waelder (1963) built on Freud's concept of overdetermination to try to explain why prediction is not possible in a complex system like the mind.

The hermeneutic trend in psychoanalysis, as represented in the work of Schafer (1992), brings the claims of developmental theories into question. Schafer takes the view that, in analysis and in other constructions of personal meaning, people's stories of their own development—their *beliefs* about the impact of past events—shape psychological life. For example, in the novel and movie *Cold Comfort Farm* (Gibbons, 1932; Schlesinger, 1996), the story generated by a grandmother's currently recalled belief that she "saw something nasty in the woodshed" shapes her own and her family's life. Belief in the developmental impact of this event, not the event itself, has a profound effect. The novel and movie are comic because the grandmother's vision of development is close to our own, that is that bad events *inevitably* affect and explain many subsequent events. Shafer's cogent idea that it is the currently told story of past events rather than the causal effects of past actualities that shapes psychological life is a major strike against Freud's developmentalism.

A second problem with the sequential developmental viewpoint in psychoanalysis is that, for specifically psychoanalytic concepts, data about the sequences of development is poor. Its primary source is the reconstruction of past occurrences, and these reconstructions are largely based on the assumption of meaningful developmental sequences. For example, the careful descriptions of individuals at the end of *Psychological Birth of the Human Infant* (Mahler et al., (1975) assume the developmental sequence they purport to demonstrate. None of the children proceeds through development in the manner predicted by the theory. Mahler and her co-workers explain the deviations, but this leaves the data in an unsatisfactory state as a support for her underlying assumptions. Unlike the biological research that led Freud to his epigenetic model, we have no equivalent of tens of thousands of slides of embryos regularly repeating developmental sequences, nor do we have clear demonstration that specific developmental lesions regularly produce specific adult pathology. In fact, we have considerable data to the contrary.

Empirical studies of early development showed expected continuities often did not occur. Kagan's (Kagan et al., 1978) pathbreaking studies of infants raised in states of severe deprivation only to emerge by age 8 as apparently healthy children led him to question the idea of continuity as the dominant theme of development and to empirically demonstrate, in a variety of contexts, that developmental discontinuities and variant paths to similar end points are common in human development (Kagan, 2000). Building on Kagan's observations and integrating them with psychoanalytic conceptualisation, Emde (1995; Emde & Spicer, 2000) has shown that developmental creativity—in essence surprising turns in development—is a central feature of normal development, especially in the face of adversity. The prospective study of psychopathology has given substantial support to the idea that discontinuity is common in development. Cicchetti (1996; Luthar et al., 2000; Cicchetti & Rogosh, 2002) has demonstrated that the absence of ordinary discontinuities can lead to pathology and that "resilience" may arise from taking a fortunate path in discontinuous developmental processes. Sameroff (1995; Sameroff & Fiese, 2000a,b) shows that the limitations of predictions based on individual and environmental factors result from the inherently complex structures of interaction between the child and infant and its environment. These complex structures are, by their nature, non-linear and exhibit significant discontinuities. Psychoanalysts are not alone in this difficulty. Reviewing the literature on psychological developmental studies of all types, Lewis (1997) observes that, while much data has been gathered to explore how presumed developmental sequences vary in populations, data supporting the existence of such sequences are rare.

The fundamental developmental model in psychoanalysis is not in a satisfactory state. It is retained because the model offers a solution to key questions about mental function by providing a picture of how it emerges. It appears to solve the glaring puzzle of how something so complex as the human psyche can exist.

Order and its genesis

When we encounter complex orderly systems, including psychological systems, an obvious question is how they came to be. Researchers in the 17th century argued for the homuncular theory of development, which posits that each germ cell contains a physical model of the mature organism with a plan for the organism's development. The theory's advocates recognised that it was problematic. (For example, the model would have to contain mini-models of all future generations.) However, these theorists were unable to think of another mechanism to transmit information about how to build an animal. In fact, lacking a general concept of information, they could not clearly formulate the problem, but struggled with it in inchoate form.

Richard Wolff, an 18th-century biologist, proposed a radically different model: epigenesis. The model postulated that development consisted in the progressive time-specific differentiation of cell types to produce mature organisms. Epigenetic models provide a way to talk about how complex organisms emerge from apparently simple beginnings. The mechanism of epigenesis remained mysterious, but the principle at least partially describes the recurring finding that new structure appears to emerge from nowhere. In today's language we would say that, in some sense, precursor cells carry the programme for the organism's development, and embryology's task is to describe that programme and how it is implemented. It is only very recently that plausible explanations have become available. The explanation of how the information moves from its encryption in the DNA molecule to the elaborate organisms we see is the current major theme of developmental biology.

The logic of the epigenetic position seems unassailable. You cannot get something for nothing. There must be a mechanism that explains the complex structures that we observe, and the only conceivable mechanism is that those structures are coded in the physical material transmitted from cell to cell. In similar fashion, it would appear unassailable that some programme for psychological development needs to be transmitted and results in personal development.

For us, epigenetic models have very much the same status that homuncular models had for those who believed in them. Because believers in homuncular theories could see no other way than the germ cell containing a small model of the mature organism by which information about mature structure could be transmitted, they were wedded to the theory. So, too, finding it impossible to conceptualise other than variations on epigenetic models by which complex order can emerge from undifferentiated beginnings, we remain committed to epigenetic models.

Another model for developmental processes

Three decades ago a new picture of the nature of processes in general began to emerge. In his amazing book *Structural Stability and Morphogeneisis: An Outline of a General Theory of Models*, Rene Thom (1975) made two observations—one mathematical and one psychological. Understanding the central mathematical idea is relatively easy. Differential equations describe how things change. Most of the laws of the physical sciences can be expressed as differential equations. Until the middle of the 20th century mathematicians focused their study on a group of equations called linear differential equations. The reason for this focus was essentially practical. A lot could be said about linear differential equations, while non-linear differential equations were very much harder to tackle. With some important exceptions, the approach to non-linear differential equations was to approximate them by linear ones, even though it was well understood that this effort was fundamentally flawed.

Linear differential equations, when used to describe the world, predict a smooth, orderly universe on every level. Their mathematics corresponded to a world that makes sense to our modern intuition—an orderly, sequential world in which effects are roughly proportionate to causes. Linear differential equations were so startlingly effective in the physical sciences that mathematician Eugene Wigner wrote a paper entitled "On the unreasonable effectiveness of mathematics" (1960).

Thom's mathematical result was the description of the fundamental configuration of certain types of non-linear differential equations in their own right, not as approximations of linear differential equations. He found that these equations did not describe a smooth, orderly world, but rather a world that was fundamentally jumpy and disorderly—although jumpy and disorderly in an orderly way. To emphasise the qualitatively different, jumpy, disorderly world described by the equations he studied, Thom humorously called the abrupt changes "catastrophes" and named his theory "catastrophe theory".

Thom's psychological discussion was also spectacular. He asserted that the "unreasonable effectiveness of mathematics" in the physical sciences does not result from a mysterious coordination of the human mind and nature, but from systematic, unconscious inattention to intractable problems. For example, the beautiful classical theory of "water waves" simply omits surf, even though every student of water waves has seen it (Stoker, 1957). The omission was not rationalised. No one said surf was unimportant or uninteresting. It was not even stated that the problem of surf was intractable and so would be put aside. When it could not be incorporated in the theory, surf became effectively invisible. Thom believes we do not perceive data for which we have no theoretical approach and, if we do not entirely ignore it, we quickly put it aside and pursue it no further. When information becomes somewhat theoretically tractable, it becomes interesting and relevant phenomena are observed.

Thom's observations apply particularly well to a discipline like psychoanalysis in which the analyst's efforts to make sense of patients' associations inevitably involve preconscious selections of the portion of the data to which the analyst attends. When data fit within a pre-existing theory they are likely to be observed but when they lie outside that theory they are not even noted by the analyst. For example, Quinodoz (1999) describes the apparently paradoxical anxiety dreams that follow periods of successful working through. In the absence of an adequate theory to explain the dynamics of these dreams they were largely understood as indicators of incomplete working through or new anxiety-arousing material emerging in the analysis. However, armed with a theory that allowed him to understand this type of dream as a capstone of the working-through process, Quinodoz was able to observe them repeatedly in analyses. Data which would otherwise have remained invisible became visible when the observer had a theory that could encompass them.

Thom's catastrophe theory was soon followed by further developments under familiar names like chaos theory, the theory of fractals and non-linear dynamical systems theory. What these points of view share is a new picture of the world that includes discontinuity, manifest disorder and jaggedness, and attention to systems that are complex (at least in comparison to the systems studied in the classical physical sciences). This new model has been applied to an ever-widening range of disciplines including history (Gaddis, 2002), the study of marriage (Gottman et al., 2002) and brain function (Haken, 2002). The major finding was that, far from being truly chaotic and disorganised, the world as studied by chaos theory is organised, but organised profoundly differently from the way we are accustomed to thinking of organisation. Furthermore, these new forms of organisation are intrinsic properties of complex systems.

A word about intuition. Many of the findings of chaos and complexity theory seem counterintuitive. However, intuitions are largely prejudices developed over time. For people in technologically advanced societies these prejudices commonly result from living in a world carefully engineered to behave in an orderly way. For example, the "intuition" that a car's acceleration is smoothly proportional to the amount of gasoline fed to the engine arises partly because automobiles are carefully engineered so that acceleration is proportional to the depression of the gas pedal. In fact, the amount of gas fed to the engine is not proportional to how far the gas pedal is depressed. Recognising that our intuition arises in a world carefully engineered to behave linearly makes the question of whether an idea is or is not intuitive less impressive. On a more psychological level, coherent personal and group narratives contribute to people's sense of organisation, effectiveness and meaning. This sense of well-being is only loosely tied to the narrative being a veridical description of the past. The shift from the medieval worldview, in which everything has meaning because everything reflects the deity's intentions, to the modern view that the physical world obeys impersonal natural laws was largely resisted because of the decreased sense of meaning inherent in the modern view (Lewis, 1964). Similarly, theories suggesting that the world often does not operate linearly, in a way consistent with current ideas of coherent narrative, are distressing and only reluctantly accepted.

Consequences of non-linear dynamics for concepts of development

What major changes in the worldview result from the chaos theory? First, we learn of a whole world of possible new structures. The great beauty of this world is now familiar in terms of fractal designs (see, for example, Mandelbrot, 1982; Barnsley, 1988; Devaney and Keen, 1989; or websites such as Sprott, 2002). Fractals are patterns of enormous complexity generated by simple rules. They usually contain elements that, on magnification, have structures qualitatively similar to but distinct from the fractal of which they form a part. Fractals are pertinent to psychoanalysis because their existence shows that structures of enormous complexity can be generated by simple rules. Elsewhere (Galatzer-Levy, 1995) I have demonstrated how the apparent complexity of obsessional symptoms can be described as built up from self similar patterns over very different time scales. The month-long oscillations of the obsessional's functioning, being composed of oscillations in attitudes, manifest time frames of about an hour, which in turn emerge from alternating attitudes lasting several minutes, which are themselves composed of speech patterns, which, over time frames of seconds, exhibit the same type of alternating positions.

Another group of structures that is important in the study of dynamical systems is "strange attractors". An attractor is a pattern of motion toward which a system tends over time. For example, if a heavenly body comes sufficiently close to the sun it will either be pulled into it, pass it by after deviating in its path of motion toward the sun, or come to orbit the sun. Each of these patterns is an attractor for the motion of body. The motion of the body need not actually follow the pattern of the attractor, but rather the motion tends toward the attractor. Descriptions of attractors often do not represent the motion directly. For example, if two similar pendulum clocks are hung on a wall together, their pendulums, after a time, will become synchronised. This synchrony is an attractor for the system of the two clocks.

Intuition—problems of which have been discussed above—suggests that systems will, over time, settle into stable patterns of relatively simple motion, such as oscillation between a small number of states. The study of non-linear dynamics demonstrates that this is often not so. There are perfectly well-defined patterns of motion that lead to sudden jumps between seemingly stable configurations. Such systems never settle into a simple pattern of motion but instead abruptly and without obvious reason shift from one pattern to a qualitatively different configuration. When a system has attractors in which abrupt qualitative changes in motion occur it is said to have strange attractors. (It should be noted that the term "motion" is used in the broad sense of change in the system and is not limited to change in position with time.) Strange attractors almost always result when the equations governing the system are non-linear.

Familiar examples of such changes include phase changes in substances. At ordinary pressures water changes from ice to liquid at 0°C and from liquid to gas (steam) at 100°C. The change is abrupt: at one temperature water is in one form, at another in the other. Given time to come to equilibrium the temperature completely determines the water's state. There are no intermediate states. From many points of view ice, liquid water and steam are qualitatively different substances, with markedly different physical properties.

The apparently qualitative shifts associated with strange attractors have broad implications for our picture of development. First, they lead us to recognise that dramatic shifts may reflect real and deep changes in configuration, not merely superficially changed manifestations. For example, the shift in psychological function that commonly occurs between ages 5 and 7 (Shapiro & Perry, 1976)—the shift into "latency"—is described from the point of view of classical theory as the manifest result of the strengthening of the superego that comes with the first resolution of the Oedipus complex and the simultaneous weakening of erotic drives. Although the resulting manifest behaviour changes, the child's underlying dynamics remain unchanged. The concept of strange attractor suggests that, rather than being simply a shift in the surface of behaviour, the shift may have resulted in an entirely new pattern of psychodynamics being in force and that the underlying pattern, as well as the superficial behaviour, have altered.

Taken further, the study of strange attractors suggests that systems may move between entirely different regimens in highly unpredictable ways, which may either be entirely intrinsic to the system or result from minuscule perturbations of it. One of the best-studied strange attractors is the Lorenz attractor, which is characterised by extended episodes of nearly periodic behaviour, which suddenly and unpredictably shift to an entirely different periodic behaviour, only to return after a time to the original periodic behaviour. In the case of the Lorenz attractor these shifts are intrinsic to the system and do not result from any perturbation at all. In toddler development it is common to see movements back and forth between clinging behaviour and vigorous assertions of autonomy. Several analytic theories characterise the shifts as resulting from conflicting, mutually incompatible motives, whose relative ascendance determines how the child behaves at a particular moment. The theory of strange attractors suggests that a better description of this situation is that the child behaviour reflects an underlying Lorenz-like attractor, with the intrinsic feature of two very different regimens and shifts between them that are intrinsic to the attractor itself. Consideration of this possibility spares us from looking for motives for shifts when intrinsic characteristics of the system lead to those shifts. It also focuses our attention on the nature of the system itself and its careful description.

The world of linear equations may be roughly characterised by the rules like: big changes have big results, small changes have small ones; and simple causes yield simple results, complex causes have complex results. The world of non linear dynamics has very different rules. Small causes *can* give very large changes; simple causes *can* yield very complex results. A popular example of small changes causing big results is a classic finding of chaos theory, the butterfly effect, that under appropriate circumstances a flap of a butterfly's wing in Sumatra can determine whether there will be a snow storm in Chicago five days later (Stewart, 2002).

Assumptions about the relationship between the intensity of cause and effect can lead analysts to misinterpret clinical data about development. A clinical example will illustrate this point. Ms. R, whose mother died during her second year, was raised by a father whose severe compulsions were interrupted by moments of extreme violence against her other caretaker, a sister five years older. As the sister moved into her teens, she became psychotically phobic and demanded Ms. R's constant attention. In late adolescence Ms. R developed progressively severe obsessional symptoms and anxiety states, including frequent panic attacks. Despite her horrendous background and continued symptoms, Ms. R did well academically and married a man who was tender, respectful and warm. In the ninth month of her pregnancy with her first child, Ms. R attended a movie. Suddenly a near-hallucinatory image of her sister and father lying in coffins appeared on the screen. At that moment her symptoms disappeared, not to return again for six years. Then her symptoms recurred with great intensity leading her to enter an analysis, which, despite lasting almost half a century, appeared to have little effect beyond holding her together at a low level of function. As she described it in a subsequent analysis with me, her analyst, a widely respected clinician, treated her sudden remission as "unreal", tried to show her that her life had not miraculously changed in a moment, and that her belief that it had resulted from an identification with her father's magical thinking was false. Because the analyst is deceased we only have the patient's statement about his attitude. However, the attitude she attributes to him is consistent with views he expressed repeatedly as a teacher. The analyst's assumptions in this regard were consistent with commonly held ideas about the proportionality of change to cause and concepts that dramatic manifest transformations are unlikely to reflect change in depth. Except that the analyst persisted in his position despite the treatment lasting so long and going so badly, some version of his position would probably be adopted by most psychoanalysts. In a subsequent analysis the analyst considered the possibility that something had really changed, that a qualitative shift in function had resulted from quantitative changes in the forces acting within her. This not only fitted better with the patient's experience and her rich description of it, but it also opened what turned out to be the therapeutically useful idea that real change was possible despite the patient's advanced age of 85. The appreciation of discontinuity, as well as continuity, and the capacity to recognise that change need not be proportionate to cause opened new analytic possibilities based on a concept of development arising from non linear dynamics.

To understand why non-linear dynamics is the appropriate framework for understanding systems like the mind we need to look briefly at the history of the mathematical understanding of the natural world. Until the middle of the 20th century, research and mathematical models were limited to those systems in which simple rules resulted in simple solutions. From Newton's demonstration that a simple law of gravitation could exist, through innumerable successes in describing physical systems over the last four centuries, scientists repeatedly showed that simple systems could be generated by even simpler laws. Much of the success of this programme resulted from focusing on real systems that could be well approximated by simple models. For example, the solar system can be described well ignoring the interactions between the planets themselves (that is, solving the problem as though only each planet's interaction with the sun mattered) and then improving the resulting solution by treating the interactions between the planets as perturbations of the resulting regular motions, which can only be of three types (Hurewicz, 1958). However, if we introduce just one more step in our discussion, asking to solve the equations that result if we try to predict the motion of three bodies under gravitation (a problem already proposed by Newton), the situation becomes mathematically intractable. Over the last forty years, it has become apparent that highly regular systems, such as Newton studied, are at one end of a spectrum that ranges from great regularity to pervasive irregularity.

The part of that spectrum that is beyond regularity was first noted to be of great practical importance by Wiener (1961), who showed that systems that include feedback are inevitably characterised by complex non-linear evolution. For a system to learn from the environment's responses to its action, feedback is essential. This is because adaptation requires change in the system. When an adaptive system is perturbed it must not simply return to its pre-perturbation state. Rather, adaptive systems must enter new states as a result of experience. Thus, any system that can "learn" is inherently unstable. The capacity to learn carries with it the risk of disorder.

Between absolute order and sheer chaos, there is an area of complexly evolving systems. If complexity and interestingness—the capacity to adapt to changing circumstances—are desired, systems must be on the edge of chaos. Because of the mathematical structure of the capacity to learn, such systems are at risk of two inherent dangers— stagnation, moving into a stable imperturbable configuration, and disorder, where all meaningful regularity is lost.

In fact, we have an example of interesting, complex systems in neural networks. Neural networks are the best models we have of real nervous-system function. They benefit and suffer from the feature that, while they are adaptive in the areas where they function well, they are not predictable nor are they reliable in the way that machines are reliable. Short of running the neural network itself, it is difficult or impossible to predict its detailed behaviour. The results of neural networks are often surprising and small shifts to their input can produce dramatic changes in the output. Neural networks can be "creative" in the sense of developing patterns not anticipated by their designers.

New learning occurs in adaptive systems on the edge of chaos, between the twin dangers of stagnation and disorganisation. This suggests that during periods of development we would expect not to see an orderly unfolding of pre-programmed structures but, instead, periods of relative disorganisation. In so far as there is any underlying programme, it would be expected to be an arrangement designed to create a situation at the edge of chaos. During periods of development people seek out stimuli and explore the world, while at the same time avoiding stimuli of traumatic (i.e. disorganising) intensity. In certain circumstances the balance would be expected to be problematic. A great deal of psychopathology can be conceptualised as resulting either from an incapacity to protect against overstimulation or a too-successful effort to avoid such stimulation with the result that little or no new experience occurs.

In terms of developmental theory, the most interesting feature of the very complex systems is their underlying simplicity. In the 19th century an argument commonly used in favour of divine creation concerned finding a watch in a desert. Were this to happen, the argument went, we would assume that there was a watch maker. The complexity of biological organisms, thus, was taken to prove God's existence. Darwin showed the fault in this argument. He demonstrated that the complexity of living organisms could result from natural selection involving no design. Natural selection is an intrinsically simple process requiring only an environment that favours one inheritable form over another. It involves no intention to create squid, bacteria, elms and people. When complex form results from a process containing no model or blueprint of that form, we speak of "emergence" and call the resulting form "emergent". Very simple rules, like natural selection, can produce very complex forms. The well-known Mandelbrot set arises from extremely simple rules, yet its form is, in a reasonable sense, infinitely complex. (See Galatzer-Levy, 2002, for a further discussion of emergence in psychoanalytic contexts.)

Non-linear dynamics suggests that development can occur by other means than epigenetic unfolding of predetermined developmental lines. In a non-linear system configurations need not be specified in advance. The rules generating highly complex systems may be very simple and their relationship to the final structure obscure and unpredictable. If the system needs to adapt or to solve some problem through its ultimate structure then the end result of the evolution of the non-linear system is limited to a range of possible solutions. However, the means by which the system reached that state and the details of the ultimate state need not be specified in advance. For example, Thelen and Smith (1994) show that, although young children's walking gait solves the problem of upright locomotion within the parameters imposed by bodily structures, children learn to walk in diverse ways, none of which should be construed as a built-in plan for learning to walk. More broadly, human development may be conceptualised as resulting from certain relatively simple rules of neural network function (Spitzer, 1999) operating within the context of biological needs and individual experiences.

Many predictions based on dynamic system models differ from those based on epigenetic unfolding. These models predict that desirable development may follow many unpredictable routes to satisfactory, and often similar, outcomes. In this model new desirable structures may emerge (in the sense described above), that is, without a pre-existing prescription. Atypical development is not necessarily "off track" (in the sense of being undesirable) but should be considered as a possible unexpected developmental route. Because non-linear development is often surgent, periods where little change occurs do not necessarily represent failed development, nor should very rapid development be automatically equated with superficial or incomplete development. Finally, since development does not have an intrinsic end, that is, it is not the result of an inborn blueprint aimed at a final state, the outcome of development is only properly assessed by its practical consequences, not some pre-formed image of normalcy.

The non-linear, non-epigenetic model of development suggests a shift of analytic attention away from steps along a developmental line to the processes active in development itself. The presupposition that there must be a normal developmental line connecting early states to mature ones should be abandoned. Research exploring developmental lines must be re-examined with an eye to the question of whether the assumption of the line's existence led to distorted interpretation, the data by which, for example, very different processes were artificially lumped together and described as representing variations on a single process. For example, the shift from relative reliance on caretakers to relative independence that occurs during the toddler period has, at various times, been seen as a derivative of the anal phase, a manifestation of separation–individuation, or a change in the nature of attachment, to name but a few. The beginning and end of the process are fairly clear and easily observed but the presumptive underlying process is far from clear. While interpretation can shoe-horn almost all observations into any one of these models, the fit is often strained. In non linear systems models, unlike epigenetic models, the fact that processes share initial and end points does not indicate that the paths joining these points are the same. Instead it leaves us free, in each case, to explore the path taken by the individual and suggests that there will often be multiple paths between various developmental points. The analyst confronted with a patient who frantically clings to potential caregivers for support needs no longer ask which developmental line is interrupted because multiple pathways can lead to the phenomena of relative independence. Similarly, the question of how the patient may be helped to resume development along the path that was earlier interrupted becomes inappropriate and the quandaries it raises (for example, how the adult analytic patient can be provided with experiences that promote imfamts' development) may be put aside. Recognising that multiple developmental pathways can have essentially similar ends and that the freedom to experience and develop is the core contributor to needed development, the analyst will no longer focus on how to get the patient back on a prescribed developmental path, but rather on creating an environment that permits optimal disorganisation in which the patient may find novel means for moving forward.

Environmental influences can be more easily integrated into a non-linear systems model than they can into epigenetic models. In epigenetic models environmental influences ordinarily complement the unfolding internal programme by providing needed supplies for the pre-programmed intrinsic process (Winnicott, 1960b, 1965; Green, 1975). In the epigenetic model, pathology results when the environment either fails to provide needed supplies or distorts the epigenetic process by exposing the child to experiences that turn it away from normal development. In contrast, non-linear models predict that input from the environment, while essential for development and shaping it, need not complement some pre-existing plan. It only needs to provide sufficiently rich experience that the system can become organised under its influence and a sufficiently calm environment that the developing individual is not thrown into chaos. Experiences will shape resulting development but how they influence its development is not predictable. In particular, experiences that are generally regarded as untoward may, in this model, lead to desirable developments not because the damaging consequences are overcome but because the experience is initially integrated into the neural network in a fashion that leads to improved functioning. Phenomena like "resilience", in which individuals do well despite being exposed to situations that would be presumed to damage development, do not require a special mechanism to explain them. Rather the phenomena reflect the same underlying mechanism that leads to desirable outcomes. The relative absence of experience leads to stagnation in neural networks so that the model would predict that environmental deprivation, such as occurs, for example, in maternal depression, would be likely to have particularly negative effects on the developing child. It may be that traumatic events actually operate to decrease the input to higher cortical functioning. Sufficiently intense danger results in an interference with the use of cortical processing in favour of more rapid emergency emotional system processing (LeDoux, 1996). Thus, in trauma, the cortical network may be deprived of experience despite the intensity of the external event. Because, once operating in this mode, information reminiscent of the traumatic event sets off processes that continue to block cortical processing of the information, trauma may result in substantially reduced cortical input and operate like deprivation in development.

Even extremely dreadful events, if integrated into the personality, may have stable and valuable developmental consequences. A historical example may be used to illustrate this point. Sixteen-year-old Sojourner Truth, a slave in Upstate New York in the 1830s, passively idealised her owner who had promised to keep Sojourner's family intact. When he sold family members, Sojourner had an apocalyptic experience. Lasting a brief time, it involved an initial sense of profound disappointment, a sudden realisation of the presence of God in her life and a commitment to struggle for the abolition of slavery. This experience appeared to have effected a lasting transformation in her personality that permitted her to act consistently, vigorously and effectively over six decades to achieve her goals as a major leader, first of the abolitionist and then the feminist movements (Gilbert, 1993; Mabee, 1993; Painter, 1996). A complex, apparently structural change emerged in minutes. The sceptical reader is likely to say that this change must have rested on earlier positive experiences and, indeed, Sojourner's very bleak childhood seems to have included the loving care of her mother. But the reader should also consider the possibility, based on a non-linear dynamics model, that the character-logic shift described was as dramatic and stable as Sojourner claimed it was.

A non-linear dynamic system model applies particularly well to systems involving two or more individuals whose developments interact. The idea that developmental processes affect not only the child but also the caretaker was first introduced by Benedek (1959), who suggested that, as children pass through various developmental stages, their parents re-engage and rework the psychological issues of that period. Subsequent studies, especially of early development, have shown that the caretaker–infant influence is typically bidirectional and is often best described as some sort of synchronisation of parent–child function (see, for example, Stern, 1985; Wolff, 1987). Analysts and infant researchers have been challenged to find ways to describe these complex interactions, which involve a kind of mutual entrainment of schedules and actions. Coupled oscillators (two oscillators, each with its own properties, which have been joined together into a single system by connecting them) have long interested mathematicians and students of dynamical systems. The coupled oscillator system provides a model of the child–caretaker (or analyst–analysand) system. A simple example of coupled oscillators is two pendulums joined by an elastic band.

It is beyond the scope of this paper to describe the possible configurations of coupled oscillators. However, some of their more interesting features include the way in which they come to form regular patterns of motion, the fact that these patterns often involve complex motions, and that neither oscillator may come to a stable state but instead may move between various states. For example, the oscillators may come to alternate high amplitudes of oscillation. The joining of two oscillators results in the emergence of patterns not only for the system as a whole but for each of the oscillators that would be impossible without this coupling. Many of the properties of dynamic systems depend on their dimension, that is, the numbers of variables that can change independently of one another (for example, a train running along a track operates in one dimension because its position is determined by one parameter; the shoulder joint is a two-dimensional system because its state is described by two parameters). Phenomena that are impossible in a system of a lower dimension become possible in systems of higher dimensions. The joining together of two

individuals into a single unit for the purposes of development effectively creates a higher-dimensional structure in which changes,
impossible in the lower-dimensional configuration, become possible.
The joining together of child and caretaker effectively produces such
a higher-dimensional system, which then allows development in ways
that neither person alone could achieve. This may be one reason the
caretaker's psychological investment in a particular child and the
development of attunement between child and caretaker is so important. Rather than simply providing responsiveness to the child's
independently generated developmental needs, we can conceptualise
the relationship as resulting in a new system whose dynamic properties are more than the sum of the properties of the infant and caretaker
separately. (Again, the extension of these ideas to the analytic dyad is
obvious.)

Clinical implication

The most important things that can go wrong with a complex system
are stagnation and disorganisation. These can be thought of as consti-
tuting two major forms of psychopathology. They also constitute the
dialectic that constantly worries people. Fear of disorganisation
commonly leads to defensively stable but maladaptive solutions.
Inadequately stable functional configurations make finding personal
meaning, comfort and satisfying relations with others difficult.

Analytic theories of development have tended to focus on the various problems people confront and the various solutions they use,
rather than on the *process* of solution. It is within this context that the
various developmental charts discussed earlier were drawn. Such
charts are misleading because they suggest orderly sequential psychological steps in normal development, and that the goal of analysis
should be conceptualised primarily in terms of movement with regard
to those steps.

I suggest that the core feature of normal developmental situations
(and, by extension, a central aspect of the analytic set-up) lies in the
ability to construct a general context for problem solution. Problem
solution is characterised principally by the re-establishment of function within the area of complexity, that is, within the area where
more complicated development remains possible as opposed to stasis

or disorganisation, in the area characterised in studies of complex systems as "on the edge of chaos". This development need not be according to some elaborate preordained plan we call normal.

It is development *per se* that is central to both health and cure. We may think of development as associated with two factors: one being the adaptational challenge faced by the person, the other the capacity to maintain work within the area of complexity. Problematic or failed development results when the individual lacks the freedom to explore configurations of function in a sufficiently disorganised way that new possibilities can emerge.

Mr M had been an extraordinarily good boy, well liked by parents, teachers and friends, all of whom he pleased with his warm consideration. He had a set of elaborate rituals that he needed to perform before sleeping and after using the toilet. These involved keeping "everything in order". As he passed through adolescence and young adulthood his superficially pleasant manner continued to make him popular with others but he had an increasing sense of angry frustration that he was not really living a life. Efforts at intimacy were either entirely aborted by inhibition about approaching women or ended after he joylessly engaged in a "normal" sexual act. He sought analysis because life seemed an endless series of meaningless performances. Although specific anxieties soon became clear during the analytic work, the overarching theme of the analysis was the way in which Mr M responded to any emotionally novel situation by identifying a "normal" response and attempting to engage it. No unsolved problems were permitted and, not surprisingly, no genuinely new solutions had emerged since the latency "good boy" posture had been adopted. Mr M could never allow himself near the "edge of chaos" and so was doomed to forever repeat his traditional limited solutions of all manner of psychological challenges.

Just as a non-linear model of development predicts that in many situations there will be long periods of manifest inactivity followed by dramatic developmental change, so, too, it predicts that developmental processes will not operate by the slow accretion of change but that the process will, in many instances, be characterised by shifts that are preliminary to an abrupt and qualitative change in function. This means that both in development and the analytic situation (Palombo, 1999) abrupt change should not be treated as in any sense unreal but should be recognised as a common way in which change occurs in complex systems.

Consistent with linear models of development, analysts tend to listen for evidence of continuity in the narratives of subjects' lives. They attempt to show how earlier, if previously unconscious, aspects of character became manifest or were uncovered in apparently abrupt processes. This attitude minimises the significance of the manifest apparently abrupt change. It puts aside the question of why and how the change occurred abruptly and even suggests that the appearance of abruptness is an illusion. Ignoring the manifest discontinuity, or putting it aside as an epiphenomenon, reflects not only an appreciation of unconscious processes but also the adoption of a linear world-view that assumes continuity and proportionality of cause and effect. Putting aside assumptions appropriate to linear systems opens up the question of whether these abrupt but lasting changes in manifest function represent significant reorganisation of the personality (i.e. structural change). The focus of investigation shifts from the limited search for latent continuities to questions such as whether, in appropriate circumstances, people's minds can become significantly disorganised and then successfully reorganised, or whether, in a particular circumstance, a dramatic shift in underlying function has occurred.

Reducing the status of the various epigenetic sequences to mere descriptions of ways people have commonly dealt with the biological and social situations that confront them, and understanding the history that we hear and reconstruct in the psychoanalytic situation as largely shaped by the use of the history in the present rather than past events, we open the possibility of exploring non-linear processes in normal development and psychoanalysis. Non-linear models have the advantage that they better fit the data of development and suggest an approach to therapeutics that avoids the implicit expectation that the process will result in the approximation of a putatively normal development sequence. Phenomena like qualitative shifts in functioning and non-pathological variation in development and mature function fit within the theory. It suggests an approach to therapeutics in which the major work of the analyst is to provide an environment in which development can be resumed in safety, rather than an attempt to achieve any particular developmental aim.

References

Abraham, K. (1924). A short study of the development of the libido, viewed in the light of mental disorders. In: *Selected Papers of Karl Abraham, M.D.* (pp. 418–501). London: Hogarth Press.

Barnsley, M. (1988). *Fractals Everywhere.* Boston, MA: Academic Press.

Benedek, T. (1959). Parenthood as a developmental phase. In: *Psychoanalytic Investigations* (pp. 378–401). New York: Quadrangle, 1973.

Blos, P. (1941). *The Adolescent Personality: A Study of Individual Behavior for the Commission on Secondary School Curriculum.* New York: Appleton Century Kauft.

Blos, P. (1962). *On Adolescence: A Psychoanalytic Interpretation.* New York: Free Press of Glencoe.

Blos, P. (1967). The second individuation process of adolescence. *Psychoanalytic Study of the Child, 22*: 162–186.

Blos, P. (1968). Character formation in adolescence. *Psychoanalytic Study of the Child, 23*: 245–263.

Case, R. (1992). *The Mind's Staircase: Exploring the Conceptual Underpinnings of Children's Thought and Knowledge.* Hillside, NJ: Lawrence Erlbaum.

Cicchetti, D. (1996). Developmental theory: lessons from the study of risk and psychopathology. In: A. Matthysse & D. Levy (Eds.), *Psychopathology: The Evolving Science of Mental Disorder* (pp. 253–284). New York: Wiley.

Cicchetti, D., & Rogosch, F. (2002). A developmental psychopathology perspective on adolescence. *Journal of Consulting Clinical Psychology, 70*: 6–20.

Devaney, R., & Keen, L (1989). *Chaos and Fractals: The Mathematics behind the Computer Graphics.* Providence, RI: American Mathematical Society.

Dusheck, J. (2002). The interpretations of genes. *Natural History, 111*: 52–59.

Emde, R. N. (1995). Diagnosis, assessment, and individual complexity. *Archives of General Psychiatry, 52*: 637–638.

Emde, R. N., & Spicer, P. (2000). Experience in the midst of variation: new horizons for development and psychopathology. *Developmental Psychopathology, 12*: 313–331.

Erikson, E. (1958). *Young Man Luther: A Study in Psychoanalysis and History.* New York: Norton.

Erikson, E. (1963). *Childhood and Society* (2nd edn). New York: Norton.

Erikson, E. (1964). *Insight and Responsibility.* New York: Norton.

Erikson, E. (1968). *Identity: Youth and Crisis.* New York: Norton.

Erikson, E. (1978). *Adulthood.* New York: Norton.

Erikson, E. (1982). *The Life-cycle Completed: A Review*. New York: Norton.

Erikson, E. (1984). Reflections on the last stage—and the first. *Psychoanalytic Study of the Child*, 39: 155–165.

Fonagy, P., & Target, M. (2003). *Psychoanalytic Theories: Perspectives from Developmental Psychopathology*. New York: Brunner Routledge.

Freud, A. (1958). Adolescence. In: *The Writings of Anna Freud, Vol. 5* (pp. 136–66). New York: International Universities Press.

Freud, A. (1965). *Normality and Pathology in Childhood: Assessments of Development*. New York: International Universities Press.

Freud, S. (1905d). *Three Essays on the Theory of Sexuality. S. E.*, 7: 125–245. London: Hogarth.

Freud, S. (1908b). Character and anal erotism. *S. E.*, 9: 169–175. London: Hogarth.

Freud, S. (1909b). *Analysis of a Phobia in a Five-year-old Boy. S. E.*, 10: 3–149. London: Hogarth.

Freud, S. (1914c). On narcissism: an introduction. *S. E.*, 14: 73–102. London: Hogarth.

Freud, S. (1916–1917). *Introductory Lectures on Psycho-analysis. S. E.*, 15–16. London: Hogarth.

Freud, S. (1923b). *The Ego and the Id. S. E.*, 19: 3–66. London: Hogarth.

Freud, S. (1926d). *Inhibitions, Symptoms and Anxiety. S. E.*, 20: 77–174. London: Hogarth.

Freud, S. (1940a). *An Outline of Psycho-analysis. S. E.*, 23: 141–207. London: Hogarth.

Gaddis, J. (2002). *The Landscape of History: How Historians Map the Past*. Cambridge, MA: Harvard University Press.

Galatzer-Levy, R. (1995). Psychoanalysis and dynamical systems theory: prediction and self similarity. *Journal of the American Psychoanalytic Association*, 43: 1085–1114.

Galatzer-Levy, R. (2002). Emergence. *Psychoanalytic Inquiry*, 22: 708–727.

Galatzer-Levy, R., & Cohler, B. (1990). The developmental psychology of the self: a new worldview in psychoanalysis. *Annual of Psychoanalysis*, 18: 1–43.

Galatzer-Levy, R., & Cohler, B. (1993). *The Essential Other: A Developmental Psychology of the Self*. New York: Basic Books.

Gedo, J., & Goldberg, A. (1973). *Models of the Mind: A Psychoanalytic Perspective*. Chicago, IL: University of Chicago Press.

Gibbons, S. (1932). *Cold Comfort Farm*. New York: Longmans, Green.

Gilbert, O. (1993). *The Narrative of Sojourner Truth*. New York: Vintage.

Gottman, J., Murray, J., Swanson, C., Tyson, R., & Swanson, K. (2002). *The Mathematics of Marriage: Dynamic Non-linear Models*. Cambridge, MA: MIT Press.

Gould, S. (1977). *Ontogeny and Phylogeny*. Cambridge, MA: Harvard University Press.

Green, A. (1975). The analyst, symbolization and absence in the analytic setting (on changes in analytic practice and analytic experience). In memory of D. W. Winnicott. *International Journal of Psychoanalysis, 56*: 1–22.

Haken, H. (2002). *Brain Dynamics: Synchronization and Activity Patterns in Pulse-coupled Neural Nets with Delays and Noise*. Berlin: Springer.

Henderson, J. (1980). On fathering (the nature and functions of the father role). Part II: Conceptualization of fathering. *Canadian Journal of Psychiatry, 25*: 413–431.

Hurewicz, W. (1958). *Lectures on Ordinary Differential Equations*. Cambridge, MA: MIT Press.

Jung, C. G. (1933). *Modern Man in Search of a Soul*. New York: Harcourt, Brace and World.

Jung, C. G. (1954). *The Development of Personality*. Princeton, NJ: Princeton University Press.

Kagan, J. (2000). *Three Seductive Ideas*. Cambridge, MA: Harvard University Press.

Kagan, J., Kearsley, R., & Zelazo, P. (1978). *Infancy: Its Place in Human Development*. Cambridge, MA: Harvard University Press.

Klein, M. (1923). The development of a child. *International Journal of Psychoanalysis, 4*: 419–474.

Klein, M. (1928). Early stages of the Oedipus conflict. *International Journal of Psycho-Analysis, 9*: 167–180.

Klein, M. (1935). A contribution to the psychogenesis of manic-depressive states. *International Journal of Psycho-Analysis, 16*: 145–174.

Klein, M. (1937). Love, guilt and reparation. In: *Love, Guilt and Reparation and Other Works, 1927–1945* (pp. 344–369). New York: Delacorte Press/Seymour Lawrence.

Klein, M. (1945). The Oedipus complex in the light of early anxieties. In: *Love, Guilt and Reparation and Other Works, 1927–1945* (pp. 370–419). New York: Delacorte Press/Seymour Lawrence,.

Klein, M. (1957). *Envy and Gratitude*. London: Tavistock.

Klein, M. (1969). *The Psychoanalysis of Children*. London: Hogarth.

Kohut, H. (1966). Forms and transformations of narcissism. *Journal of the American Psychoanalytic Association, 14*: 243–272.

Kohut, H (1971). *The Analysis of the Self*. New York: International Universities Press.

Kohut, H. (1977). *The Restoration of the Self*. New York: International Universities Press.

LeDoux, J. (1996). *The Emotional Brain*. New York: Simon & Schuster.

Lewis, C. (1964). *The Discarded Image: An Introduction to Medieval and Renaissance Literature*. Cambridge: Cambridge University Press.

Lewis, M. (1997). *Altering Fate: Why the Past Does Not Predict the Future*. New York: Guilford Press.

Lichtenberg, J. (1975). The development of the sense of self. *Journal of the American Psychoanalytic Assocciation, 23*: 453–484.

Lichtenberg, J. (1979). Factors in the development of the sense of the object. *Journal of the American Psychoanalytic Association, 27*: 375–386.

Lichtenberg, J. (1983). *Psychoanalysis and Infant Research*. Hillsdale, NJ: Analytic Press.

Luthar, S., Cicchetti, D., & Becker, B. (2000). The construct of resilience: a critical evaluation and guidelines for future work. *Child Development, 71*: 543–562.

Mabee, C. (1993). *Sojourner Truth: Slave, Prophet, Legend*. New York: New York University Press.

Mahler, M. (1952). On child psychosis and schizophrenia: autistic and symbiotic infantile psychoses. *Psychoanalytic Study of the Child, 7*: 286–305.

Mahler, M. (1958). Autism and symbiosis: Two extreme disturbances of identity. *International Journal of Psychoanalysis, 39*: 77–83.

Mahler, M. (1968). *On Human Symbioses and the Vicissitudes of Individuation. Vol 1: Infantile Psychosis*. New York: International Universities Press.

Mahler, M. (1971). A study of the separation–individuation process and its possible application to borderline phenomena in the psychoanalytic situation. *Psychoanalytic Study of the Child, 26*: 403–424.

Mahler, M. (1972). On the first three subphases of the separation–individuation process. *International Journal of Psychoanalysis, 53*: 333–338.

Mahler, M., Pine, F., & Bergman, A. (1975). *The Psychological Birth of a Human Infant*. New York: Basic Books.

Mandelbrot, B. (1982). *The Fractal Geometry of Nature*. San Francisco, CA: Freeman.

Needham, J. (1959). *A History of Embryology* (2nd edn). New York: Abelard-Schuman.

Painter, N. (1996). *Sojourner Truth: A Life, a Symbol*. New York: Norton.

Palombo, S. (1999). *The Emergent Ego: Complexity and Coevolution in the Psychoanalytic Process*. Madison, CT: International Universities Press.

Panel (1973a). Separation–individuation: adolescence, maturity. *Journal of the American Psychoanalytic Assocciation*, 21: 155–167.

Panel (1973b). Separation–individuation: maturity, senescence. *Journal of the American Psychoanalytic Assocciation*, 21: 633–645.

Quinodoz, J.-M. (1999). Dreams that turn over a page. *International Journal of Psychoanalysis, 80*: 225–238.

Rangell, L. (1989). Rapprochement and other crises. The specific and nonspecific in analytic reconstruction. *Psychoanalytic Study of the Child*, 44: 19–39.

Reich, W. (1949). *Character Analysis* (3rd edn). New York: Farrar, Straus & Giroux.

Reich, W. (1975). *Early Writings*. New York: Farrah, Strauss, Giraux.

Sameroff, A. (1995). General systems theories and developmental psychopathology. In: D. Cicchetti & D. Cohen (Eds.), *Developmental Psychopathology, Vol. 1: Theory and Methods* (pp. 659–695). New York: Wiley.

Sameroff, A., & Fiese, B. (2000a). Transactional regulation: the developmental ecology of early intervention. In: J. Shonkoff & S. Meisels (Eds.), *Handbook of Early Childhood Intervention* (2nd edn) (pp. 135–159). New York: Wiley.

Sameroff, A., & Fiese, B. (2000b). Models of development and developmental risk. In: C. H. Zeanah Jr (Ed.), *Handbook of Infant Mental Health* (2nd edn) (pp. 3–19). New York: Wiley.

Schafer, R. (1973). Concepts of self and identity and the experience of separation–individuation in adolescence. *Psychoanalytic Quarterly, 42*: 42–59.

Schafer, R. (1976). Concepts of self and identity in relation to separation–individuation. In: *A New Language for Psychoanalysis*. New Haven, CT: Yale University Press.

Schafer, R. (1992). *Retelling a Life: Narration and Dialogue in Psychoanalysis*. New York: Basic Books.

Schlesinger, J. (Director) (1996). *Cold Comfort Farm*. London: BBC.

Shapiro, T., & Perry, R. (1976). Latency revisited. The age 7 plus or minus 1. *Psychoanalytic Study of the Child, 31*: 79–105.

Spitzer, M. (1999). *The Mind Within the Net*. Cambridge, MA: MIT Press.

Sprott, J. (2002). Sprott's fractal factory. http://sprott.physics.wisc.edu/fractals.htm.

Stern, D. (1985). *The Interpersonal World of the Infant*. New York: Basic Books.

Stewart, I. (2002). *Does God Play Dice?* (2nd edn). New York: Blackwell.

Stoker, J. (1957). *Water Waves*. New York: Wiley.

Sulloway, S. (1979). *Freud, Biologist of the Mind: Beyond the Psychoanalytic Legend*. New York: Basic Books.

Thelen, E., & Smith, L. (1994). *A Dynamic Systems Approach to the Development of Cognition and Action*. Cambridge, MA: MIT Press.

Thom, R. (1975). *Structural Stability and Morphogeneisis: An Outline of a General Theory of Models*. Reading: Benjamin.

Waelder, R. (1963). Psychic determinism and the possibility of predictions. *Psychoanalytic Quarterly, 32*: 15–42.

Wiener, N. (1961). *Cybernetics or the Control and Communication in Animal and the Machine* (2nd edn). Cambridge, MA: MIT Press.

Wigner, E. (1960). The unreasonable effectiveness of mathematics in the natural sciences. *Communications on Pure and Applied Mathematics, 13*: 1–14.

Winnicott, D. W. (1945–1958). Primitive emotional development. In: *Collected Papers: Through Pediatrics to Psychoanalysis* (pp. 145–156). New York: Basic Books.

Winnicott, D. W. (1953). Transitional objects and transitional phenomena. In: *Collected Papers: Through Pediatrics to Psychoanalysis* (pp. 229–242). New York: Basic Books.

Winnicott, D. W. (1958). The capacity to be alone. In: *The Maturational Process and the Facilitating Environment* (pp. 29–36). New York: International Universities Press.

Winnicott, D. W. (1960a). Ego distortion in terms of the true and false self. In: *The Maturational Process and the Facilitating Environment* (pp. 140–152). New York: International Universities Press.

Winnicott, D. W. (1960b). The theory of the parent–infant relationship. *International Journal of Psychoanalysis, 41*: 585–595.

Winnicott, D. W. (1962). The aims of psycho-analytic treatment. In: *The Maturational Process and the Facilitating Environment*. London: Hogarth Press.

Winnicott, D. W. (1963a). From dependence towards independence in the development of the individual. In: *The Maturational Process and the Facilitating Environment* (pp. 83–92). New York: International Universities Press.

Winnicott, D. W. (1963b). Psychiatric disorder in terms of infantile maturational processes. In: *The Maturational Process and the Facilitating Environment* (pp. 230–241). New York: Basic Books.

Winnicott, D. W. (1965). *The Maturational Process and the Facilitating Environment*. New York: International Universities Press.

Wolff, P. (1987). *The Development of Behavioral States and the Expression of Motion in Early Infancy*. Chicago. IL: University of Chicago Press.

PART II

CLINICAL AND TECHNICAL IMPLICATIONS OF THE NON-LINEAR MODEL

Introduction to Part II

The second part of the book is concerned with the technical application of the ideas of chaos theory to the understanding of therapeutic action and psychic change. In part, this is in terms of how the iterative nature of the psychoanalytic procedure allows the strange attractors governing someone's psychic life to emerge into consciousness and become observable by both patient and his psychoanalyst. With this can be said to come the possibility of choice but it is often a long road. This is because these strange attractors reflect how the individual has developed and learned to cope with the "slings and arrows of outrageous fortune". Change inevitably brings the anxiety of loss—in particular the loss of control, which has been hard won—in phantasy and/or reality as the subject has grown and developed.

Looking back over the papers reproduced so far, the reader might feel that another reason for the interest in chaos theory is that it offers the prospect of healing the split referred to above by Whittle. This is because the method necessary for the investigation of experience assumes that it cannot be understood in the immediate. It is only over time that the *patterns* of experience can be observed within an iterative learning system. This enables us to deepen our understanding of the psychoanalytic process through the examination of the properties of iterative systems. The implication is that we are not forced by the unique quality of the analysis of any one person to treat it as a phenomenon that cannot be compared with another. While any one individual is unique—just as their analysis will be—this does not mean that the process by which the analysis is conducted is idiosyncratic and incomparable to other analytic experiences. By thinking about the mind, and the means of studying it, as being non-linear systems, we can do justice to the reality of the complexity of what we are studying and have an instrument – the psychoanalytic iterating learning system—which is, as it were, "fit for purpose" in the study of the mind's complexity. Of course, the experience that psychoanalysts have gained from the work has enabled various generalisations to be made about the features of all human subjects. These are made manifest by the different meta-psychologies that have emerged over the past century. However, ultimately this book proposes that the study of the process of psychoanalytic investigation using the concepts derived from chaos theory offers the prospect of becoming more objective about the experience of subjectivity.

This part of the book begins with a clinical chapter by Graham Shulman. It concentrates on clinical application of these ideas and looks at how the notion of the strange attractor helps to describe the quality of repetition of the psychic phenomena described. Thus, it helps to organise the data emerging from the psychoanalytic learning system. He considers some detailed clinical material to show how "the damaged object" in a child's mind acts as a strange attractor. He further explores the implications for thinking about therapeutic action.

The next chapter is by James Rose, who seeks to use these ideas to think about the effectiveness of varying numbers of sessions per week in revealing a patient's psychic structure. In this chapter, Rose explores the nature of the iterative learning system, which is created when a psychoanalytic treatment is begun. In this latter part of the book, the relevance of these ideas to practising psychoanalysts and psychoanalytic psychotherapists is demonstrated.

CHAPTER FIVE

Internal objects considered as strange attractors in the non-linear dynamical system of the mind*

Graham Shulman

> But men may construe things after their fashion,
> Clean from the purpose of the things themselves.
>
> (William Shakespeare)

I n this chapter, I discuss a specific set of circumstances in which the damaged internal object can exercise a perturbing and determining influence on the relationship to reality and the development of the capacity to differentiate internal and external reality. Drawing on the concept of the strange attractor from chaos theory, I suggest that the damaged object in such circumstances operates as a strange attractor in the mind. I describe a clinical case of once weekly psychoanalytic psychotherapy with a seven-year-old child to illustrate these themes.

The conjunction of internal and external realities

The lines from Shakespeare which I have used as an epigraph to this chapter encapsulate a core dimension of the psychoanalytic field of

* Material from this chapter was originally published in the *Journal of Child Psychotherapy*, 36(3): 259–288 and is reproduced with permission of Taylor & Francis Ltd.

enquiry: that is, the ways in which people may unconsciously "construe things after their fashion" in terms of their "purpose"/ meaning in both the internal and external world. The development of the sense of reality, and, in particular, the differentiation of internal and external reality, has its roots in early infancy and is a gradual, fluctuating, and never absolute achievement. Problems in the differentiation of internal and external reality may arise for a variety of reasons. Most common in the psychoanalytic literature is the theme of confusion of internal and external reality consequent upon excessive projective identification (Bion, 1962, p. 32). I shall consider another source of difficulty in the differentiation of internal and external reality, associated with the effects of the damaged object in a particular constellation of internal and external worlds.

Developmental psychology research has been instrumental in showing how, from birth, infants have the capacity to relate to, interact with, and elicit responses from their mother and significant others, in motivated, purposeful, and meaningful ways. This research demonstrates that infants have a clear perception and understanding of, and relationship to, *selective* aspects of external reality and the environment. The research also confirms the infant's understanding of causation *within circumscribed areas of perception and experience.*

Alvarez and Furgiuele (1997), drawing in part on developmental psychology research (Bruner, 1968; Papousek & Papousek, 1975; Tompkins, 1981; Trevarthen & Hubley, 1978) as well as from psychoanalytic writing on this theme (Broucek, 1979, 1991), have discussed the link between the development of the understanding of causation and the development of a sense of agency. They argue that these co-evolve through the interactions, communications, and patterns of response in the earliest mother–infant relationship. These two strands of mental and emotional development are, in turn, intimately bound up with the sense of self. To paraphrase: "I cause mother to feel and register my communications, and understand and respond to my states of mind, therefore I am".

But what inferences of causation might the developing young infant make about the connection between him- or herself and "the *state* of things in the external world"—initially, the state of other people and, first and foremost, mother or the primary attachment figure? Developmental research tells us nothing about the ways in which infants "may construe things after their fashion" in relation to *the cause of the emotional or psychological* state or condition *of people in the external world.* An obvious situation where this wider question is relevant is that of mothers with postnatal depression: in so far as the baby senses and internalises "something wrong with mummy", might the infant "construe" itself as the cause?

Given that the breast and the mother are the primary object of identification and source of integration, the conception of a damaged breast/mummy or a breast/mummy in pieces is clearly of profound significance for the infant's emotional and psychic development and sense of self and identity. Omnipotent thinking characteristic of ordinary primitive mental functioning typically gives rise to the belief of the type "I am the cause of that" even where it is not the case. This type of belief or fantasy is easily recognisable in older children who believe—sometimes consciously, sometimes unconsciously—that they are the cause of a state, or state of affairs, for example, a mother's physical ill health, or parental divorce; and it persists, in transient form, in everyday adult life when we mistakenly think we are the cause of someone else's mood or state of mind. This ordinary type of omnipotent thinking and belief may, in turn, be compounded by omnipotent thinking as a defence against terrifying helplessness and vulnerability in the face of overwhelming or catastrophic anxiety.

When external reality mirrors internal reality

I suggest that an infant's belief in itself as the cause of mother's mental state (e.g., "mummy broken") can, in certain circumstances, be the result of the operation of a particular *conjunction* of internal phantasy on the one hand, and a sense of agency (= causation) in relation to the *external* mother on the other. The point I wish to highlight is that where external reality in some way mirrors or corresponds to internal reality, the problem might not be the infant's omnipotence of thought in itself, but the fact that *its omnipotence of thought in relation to its destructiveness is not disconfirmed by external reality in the way that both Klein and Winnicott highlight is essential to the infant's ordinary development and mental health.*

In this constellation of internal and external worlds, the interaction of internal and external reality forms a dynamic process. This touches on an often polarised debate concerning the relative importance of, and emphasis given to, internal and external reality. The understanding of confusional states and of the confusion of self and object consequent upon excessive projective identification has been a fundamental and invaluable development in psychoanalytic theory and practice (Bion, 1962; Klein, 1946; Meltzer, 1992; Rosenfeld, 1952; Segal, 1957). However, I suggest this concept needs to be clearly distinguished from what might be formulated as either a failure or *collapse* in the differentiation of internal and external reality as a result of the kind of constellation or conjunction of internal and external realities I am discussing. It is important clinically to keep the two concepts of excessive projective identification *and* mirroring of internal and external realities separate in one's mind because of their relevance to an individual's sense of responsibility, anxiety, and guilt, and to the therapist's ascription and interpretation of these, both implicit and explicit, conscious and unconscious.

Before exploring these ideas with reference to clinical material, I shall first give a brief selective overview of psychoanalytic theory related to the development of the sense of reality, and then discuss the relevance and application of chaos theory and the concept of the "strange attractor" to the process I wish to elaborate.

Development of the sense of reality: a selective theoretical overview

And we are now confronted with the task of investigating the development of the relation of . . . mankind in general to reality, and in this way of bringing the psychological significance of the real external world into the structure of our theories. (Freud, 1911b, p. 218)

The "task of investigating the development of the relation . . . of mankind in general to reality" has been at the heart of psychoanalytic inquiry since its beginnings. Freud writes of "bringing the psychological significance of the real external world into the structure of our theories" in his classic paper "Formulations on the two principles of mental functioning". In Freud's model, it is only the failure of "the attempt at satisfaction by means of hallucination"—that is, "the non-occurrence of the expected satisfaction"—that gives rise to the relationship to external reality in the form of the "reality principle". This occurs, Freud suggested, when "the psychical apparatus ha[s] to decide to form a conception of the real circumstances in the external world and to endeavour to make a real alteration in them" (1911b, p. 219).

In this classical Freudian model, external reality comes to be apprehended only as a consequence of frustration of need or wish fulfilment. It is through this process that "the objectifying of the outer world" (Ferenczi, 1913) comes about. External reality is here primarily viewed in terms of something that is acted upon, in order to bring about "satisfaction". Thinking is seen to have "developed from the presentation of ideas", and in its more developed form is regarded as "an experimental kind of acting". However, Freud goes on to suggest that thinking was originally unconscious and was "*directed to the relations between the impressions of objects*" (1911b, p. 221, my emphasis).

Ferenczi (1913) elaborated on this process of the shift to the apprehension of external reality. Ferenczi introduced the idea of "stages in the development of the sense of reality". He argued that the development of the sense of external reality is a gradual process, albeit with clearly defined stages, and, like Freud, he stressed that it is never an absolute achievement. Ferenczi highlighted the importance of a realistic relationship to external reality, and the link between certain forms of mental illness and disturbances in the differentiation of internal and external reality.

The development of the relationship to external reality and the outer world is a central theme in Klein's writings. Klein (1932, p. 11) was from the outset interested in "the child's relation to reality". She argued that the young infant's relation to external reality was coloured and shaped by phantasy (unconscious fantasy). She further suggested that symbolism is not only "the foundation of all phantasy and sublimation" but, over and above this, that it is "the basis of the subject's relation to the outside world and to reality in general" (Klein, 1930, p. 221). In Klein's view, "the child's earliest reality is wholly phantastic", but "[a]s the ego develops, a true relation to reality is gradually established out of this unreal reality" (Klein, 1930, p. 221).

Klein (1935, p. 285) drew attention to the fundamental importance of the infant's "good relation to its mother and to the external world" as a protection against "early paranoid anxieties". She highlighted the critical role of external reality in *disconfirming* internal anxieties and phantasies related to destruction or damage resulting from early destructive and sadistic attacks on the internal object. Thus she wrote: "The extent to which external reality is able to disprove anxieties and sorrow relating to the internal reality varies with each individual, but could be taken as one of the criteria for normality" (Klein, 1940, p. 346).

In this context, Klein (1940, p. 346) referred to "children who are so dominated by their internal world that that their anxieties cannot be disproved and counteracted" by the positive aspects of the external world. Pursuing this line of thought, a little later in the same paper she suggests that "the psychic reality of the child is gradually influenced by every step in his progressive knowledge of external reality" (p. 347). Klein clearly regarded this disconfirmation of internal reality by external reality as critical to the development of the capacity to tolerate depressive concern and anxiety, and thus to good mental health.

The idea of variation "with each individual" in the "extent to which external reality is able to disprove anxieties and sorrow relating to the internal reality", suggests the possibility of both internal and external factors influencing this individual variation. With "children who are so dominated by their internal world that their anxieties cannot be disproved and counteracted" by the *positive* aspects of external reality, it follows that where external reality in some way mirrors or corresponds to the damage and destruction that has been done in phantasy in the internal world, this can profoundly have an impact on, or distort, the ordinary development of the relation to external reality.

Winnicott (1971) discussed the significance of the non-destruction of the external object for the development of the sense of external reality in early infancy. He argued that the infant destroys the object in phantasy and that this is a necessary part in the process of "placing the object outside the self . . . out in the world" (Winnicott, 1971, p. 107). (For Winnicott, this is a prerequisite for the development of the capacity to "use" the object.) In this context, "finding externality . . . depends on the [external] object's capacity to survive" (Winnicott, 1971, p. 107). Winnicott highlighted the role of the external mother in this developmental process: "It is an important part of what a mother does, to be the first person to take the baby through this first version of the many that will be encountered, of attack that is survived" (Winnicott, 1971, pp. 108–109).

He drew attention to the "variations . . . that arise out of the differences in experiences of . . . new born babies according to whether they are or are not carried through this very difficult phase" (Winnicott, 1971, p. 109). In this context, Winnicott considered the implications of "the object's failure to survive". Of particular relevance is Winnicott's idea of "the object's liability not to survive, *which also means to suffer change in quality, in attitude*" (1971, p. 109, my emphasis). It follows that the quality of the external mother's state of mind (e.g., depression) might be *construed* by the infant as a consequence of its destructive attacks in phantasy. One possible motivation for the infant misconstruing the cause of the external mother's state in this way is that it might feel safer to believe this, rather than merely to suffer helplessly as a result of mother's state.

Rey (1994, p. 229) considered the nature of the relationship to reality in individuals who are dominated by the need to keep alive and repair damaged objects; these individuals aim "to bring about the reparation of certain objects without which the subject's self cannot function normally and happily". Rey (1994, p. 247) observed, "In a 'normal' person there is a kind of equilibrium between the inner world of inner objects and the external world of external objects". He suggested that the task of borderline and psychotic patients—for whom the relationship to reality is severely disturbed—is "to manage to keep their damaged good objects alive in the hope of putting them right" (Rey, 1994, p. 237). One might add that where in infancy the external world of external objects in a significant way mirrors the damage in the internal world of inner objects so that they are not easily differentiated in the mind of the infant, this normal "equilibrium" between inner and external worlds cannot be established or maintained, and the normal relationship to external reality is liable to distortion.

The field of autism has been a rich source of psychoanalytic understanding regarding the theme of the damaged object and its relation to the development of the sense of reality. Tustin (1972) discovered the type of "black hole" psychotic depression in some autistic children which is linked to the phantasy of a breast with the nipple broken off; here, the phantasy of a damaged object as a result of destructive rage can lead to the most extreme consequences in the form of autistic withdrawal and isolation from people and the external world. Tustin (1972, 1990) also discussed the problems arising from the phantasy of acquiring qualities by literally "taking" them from parental figures, leading to the belief that the parents have been damaged. Haag (1985, 2000) describes the phantasy in some children with autism of mother and baby as two halves of the same body leading to the experience of bodily separateness being equated with damage to object and self. For both writers, the phantasy of the damaged object is associated with catastrophic anxieties, resulting in the relationship to external reality becoming severely distorted, disturbed or compromised.

Rhode (2004, p. 17) has discussed catastrophic primitive phantasies of destruction in some autistic children where the "child . . . confuses his mother's state of mind with what his own mouth has done" in infancy. Elsewhere, Rhode (1999, p. 90) describes a shared feature in three children on the autistic spectrum, all of whom had a seriously disturbed relation to external reality: all three children "were acutely sensitive to other people's moods, and to the possibility that they might be responsible for causing damage". Rhode (2005) also considers the situation where such anxieties and phantasies of destruction are linked to the infant's experience of damaged or dead objects in the mind of the mother (the object's damaged internal objects). Here, it is the shadow of the object's (damaged) object falling on the ego (Barrows, 1999, cited by Rhode) that can lead to disturbance in the relation to external reality. Rhode draws on Winnicott's (1967) concept of the "mirror role of the mother" to make the point that

> the baby derives its fundamental sense of existence and goodness from what it sees reflected in its mother's face . . . we are what we see. If the mother's preoccupations [or damaged internal objects] intrude excessively for too much of the time, then these are what the baby will see . . .[as a reflection of itself]. (Rhode, 2005, p. 60)

This can lead to the catastrophic internal situation of the baby feeling itself to be both the cause of, and identified with, these damaged objects in the mother's mind. The damaged object can, thus, have a primary determining influence on the mental life of the individual, and can act as a primary organiser of mental life. In this way, the damaged object takes the form of, and functions as, a strange attractor that disrupts the child's psychic development towards the separation of internal and external realities.

Case discussion: the damaged baby and the damaging baby

In the following case, the whole Green family (not their real name) were seen for the initial assessment phase, after which there was an extended period of work with parents and the referred child together. An assessment for individual psychotherapy was carried out after over a year's work with parents and Isaac, who was seven years old at the time of the psychotherapy assessment, and this led to ongoing once weekly individual psychotherapy for the child. In the initial assessment meeting with the family, it became apparent from the start that damage was an immediate and recurrent preoccupation of Isaac's parents and of Isaac, and a central theme in their lives.

Isaac's parents spoke about his early history. Isaac was the first child of his parents. The pregnancy had been straightforward with no complications. However, Isaac was born two weeks early by a difficult, protracted, and extremely painful and traumatic (for mother and undoubtedly also for baby) forceps delivery. Isaac's head was severely squashed and bruised by the forceps delivery. His parents were concerned at the time about possible physical and psychological long-term effects. They were told by medical staff that the bruising would have no permanent physical effect, that Isaac would have no memory of the experience, and that it would have no lasting impact. It was clear to me that Isaac's birth and his condition after birth were a profound trauma for parents which had never been processed, and that while they recognised this when I named it, before I did so they had not thought of it in this way or recognised it as such.

Mother and father spoke movingly of the first few weeks after the birth, when they were unable for medical reasons to hold or cuddle their baby, except to feed him. Although they did not themselves appear to have had any thoughts about depression in mother after Isaac's birth, from what they said and the way they spoke about these first few months I was left wondering about mother's emotional state at that time. I strongly suspected mother may have been at the very least in an extremely fragile state, if not actually depressed, without anyone realising or recognising it at that time.

Mother returned to full-time work when Isaac was four months old. From my understanding this was not because of financial need. Isaac was then cared for full-time during the day by a child minder who looked after another baby at the same time. Isaac's mother became pregnant when he was two-and-a-half years old, and Isaac started full-time nursery at the age of three. There were complications in the delivery of Isaac's younger twin brothers and serious concerns about their condition, which resulted in them being placed straight-away in a special care baby unit after birth. Mother did not see her newborn twin babies for the next twenty-four hours and was not allowed to touch them for two days.

Mother subsequently developed postnatal depression. Since then she had been on antidepressants for several years—with one unsuc-cessful attempt to come off them—and father expressed to me his worry about mother's emotional and mental state and his fear of her having a breakdown, though he did not use this word. I wondered whether the traumatic birth of the twins and concerns about *their* condition echoed and revived the unprocessed trauma of their expe-rience with Isaac, and tipped mother "over the edge".

In our meetings with Isaac's parents, they spoke about Isaac as if there was "something wrong" with him that needed "fixing". This persisted throughout our contact with them, giving the impression of a powerful sense of something "irreparable". In the initial assessment, they reported that Isaac often broke things at home but not deliber-ately, and from their descriptions it did sound as if this was more like clumsiness or possibly carelessness rather than active, wilful, or unconscious destructiveness. This was in contrast to their description of other times when Isaac might break something in a fit of anger and more intentionally. The following occurred in a later session with Isaac and his parents.

Isaac got out the horse from the toy box, immediately noticed that its tail was missing and briefly wondered where it might be and searched in the toy box for it—he seemed perhaps faintly troubled by the missing tail. Then he took out the hippo and commented on that not having a tail either. Father told us that Isaac is often concerned to fix things, and that he was very bothered by a recent catastrophic event, associated with the field in which Isaac's father was involved in his work, in which a number of people had died. Isaac seemed to have been troubled that his father was not able to fix things when this event had occurred.

The theme of damage appeared at the very start of Isaac's first indi-vidual psychotherapy assessment session:

First individual psychotherapy assessment session

From the beginning of the session there was a restless and very agitated quality to his manner of speech. He seemed unreachable and it felt impossible to make a connection with him.

This very agitated and restless quality was also reflected in what Isaac did: he first got out a box with a game in consisting of a plastic head with balls that are meant to be "posted" into it ... He quickly became immersed in investigating the head: there were arms on the sides and one came off and Isaac immediately said, "I've broken it" (in fact he had not—the arms are designed to come off—though I did not say this to him) and he then said, "I break things and then I can't mend them." This had the feeling of a statement about a deep-seated sense of self and of his experience.

Later, he stood all the animals together and began joining together and laying out pieces of the train track, starting with the two halves of the bridge. He made a track that enclosed all the animals he had put out. He made a long train with all the train carriages, and pushed it round the track a few times. He then disconnected the two halves of the bridge as the train reached it and said the bridge was "broken"; the train engine then went rampaging around inside the track, violently crashing into and knocking over all the animals. He explained, when I asked, that the engine was doing this "because it was angry because it couldn't carry on" (over the bridge). When I made a link with how angry he might sometimes feel when he wants to "carry on" something but cannot, this seemed to strike a chord and Isaac agreed.

This theme of damage continued in the subsequent individual psychotherapy assessment sessions.

Second individual psychotherapy assessment session

Isaac stood all the smallest animals in a group, in a circle, facing in, referring to them as "babies", and he then did the same thing with the grown-up animals. Next he laid out the train track in a complete circuit around them, saying it was to "protect" them. He took out a large dinosaur and made repeated fierce and threatening noises in the direction of the babies, moving the dinosaur a little in their direction, and he confirmed that the dinosaur wanted to get the babies and to eat them. He then made the lion and some of the other jungle animals fight off the dinosaur and lock it away in the small baby dolls' house—Isaac said it was dead, but a little later it then came back and was alive again; this sequence was repeated, but this time Isaac made the lion repeatedly hit the dinosaur and he said the lion killed the dinosaur's spirit.

A little later he got out all the cars and laid them in a continuous line on the railway track—he called these "safety" cars; however, the cars went wild—like the train engine the previous week—and knocked over all the animals; this time Isaac could not say why or what was happening. I was struck by the contrast between this session and the previous one, in terms of the feeling of the session and how it proceeded, despite Isaac, in many respects doing similar things in both sessions. This session never really acquired the more settled, focused, and calm quality of the previous one—Isaac's play seemed less coherent, more fragmented, and there was more moving from one thing to the next.

Isaac now got the cat and mouse and made the cat chase the mouse wildly: the track got completely broken up and all the animals, which he had stood up again, were knocked over once more. Isaac played out this scene of destruction in a very immersed and excited way. The feeling of Isaac's play was increasingly agitated and I was aware of it having an *intensely* agitating and disorganising impact on my mind, to the point of it becoming extremely difficult for me to think—I felt as if all my thoughts had been broken up. I had a growing inner feeling of turmoil and chaos, and at one point I made a conscious and very active effort—it took all my concentration and determination—to try to calm this escalating inner turmoil (I did not say anything to Isaac about this): *at this precise point* there was a notable decrease in Isaac's agitation. I commented on how this session felt different from last time, and how everything kept getting knocked over and broken up again and again this time. After I said this, the quality of Isaac's play changed, and he then spent some time standing all the animals up and putting the track together again to its original shape—this felt like order and calm being restored.

Note that my determined (and on this occasion successful) effort to process my overwhelming and escalating inner turmoil and disorganisation of thought appeared to lead to an immediate reduction in Isaac's agitation and destructiveness, and that what I said to him after this led to a positive shift in his state of mind. It might have been tempting to have tried to interpret or comment directly on Isaac's destructiveness, and I could easily have unwittingly done this if I had not sufficiently processed and overcome the intensely agitated and "broken up" state of mind that Isaac's play had evoked in me. Had I not sufficiently processed this, I believe my state of mind would have been communicated in the tone or "music" of my interpretation, however much I was aware of this state of mind in myself. If I had managed to formulate an interpretation about Isaac's destructiveness, I believe what Isaac would unconsciously have taken in would have been my accompanying inner feeling of "broken up thought", and that this would have been experienced by Isaac unconsciously as confirmation of the damage he causes to his object—in this case, to someone else's mind and thinking. I suspect it would also have been unconsciously experienced by Isaac as a disturbing experience of damage being got rid of and pushed back into him.

Third individual psychotherapy assessment session

Isaac took out the baby leopard and laid it carefully right in front of the mother leopard's mouth and carefully placed the end of the baby leopard's tail inside the mother's mouth. When I commented that he had done this, Isaac said it was "So that it won't be separated."

I took up this theme of not wanting to be separated and linked it to him seeing me on his own, and I asked how he feels when he is separated from his mother. Isaac said he is "sad" and that he does not like it. In the middle of this bit of conversation about not wanting to be separated from his mother, Isaac suddenly said, "I hate my mother": this verbal outburst felt as if it just popped out as part of a stream of thoughts; it did not form part of the sentence he was in the middle of or follow (consciously) from what he had actually been saying, and he did not elaborate, but instead continued with what he had been speaking about. I picked up on what he had said, and when I asked about him feeling this he said it "happens all the time".

Isaac had by then finished standing up all the animals. While we were talking he had joined engines and carriages together on the track to make one long train, and now he said, "There's a storm'" and, unhooking the two halves of the railway track bridge that are joined in the middle, he moved them apart and said, "They're separated." He pushed the engine at the front of the train right up to the edge of where the bridge was divided in two, and said "The train can't go over."

He pushed the two halves of the bridge together so that the links were touching but not actually linked together, and said the bridge was "fixed"; when I commented on the two sections of bridge not being properly joined, and wondered whether the train would be able to get across, he said the bridge was "fixed enough" for the train to get across. I queried this but he ignored me. He began slowly edging the train across the not-properly-joined-up-middle of the bridge, then suddenly he made the train wildly smash into the bridge and break up the track. Isaac excitedly broke up the track completely and said, "It's demolished." He began moving all the animals—which had got knocked over and scattered as the track was smashed up—to the space underneath a nearby chair, carefully standing and lining them all up and saying that they "will have to stay there until their home [i.e., the track] is fixed".

I said the animals' home getting "demolished" and needing to be rebuilt reminded me of what his parents had said (in a meeting all together before the individual assessment sessions) about the building works at their home and that he was getting a new bedroom—he was having to sleep in a different room until the work on his new bedroom was finished; Isaac replied with feeling that his old room is "demolished" and that they are putting stairs where his room had been. He said he does not want to move and had wanted to stay in his old room. I suggested that he does not like changes and Isaac agreed—I thought this really struck a chord for him. I spoke here about the baby Isaac who might have wanted to stay in his mummy's tummy and not "move" or come out; Isaac spontaneously replied with feeling, "That was my home." I linked this to his dislike of being separated from his mother and being away from her. Around here, Isaac made a comment that he "hates" school, and I commented on school being another experience of being separated and away from mother and father, too; I talked about how a part of him hates being separated from his mother, and that he sometimes hates his mother for the two of them being separated.

In a subsequent session in his therapy, Isaac told me that he had "demolished" the previous house that the family had lived in when he was very young before his twin brothers were born, and that this was the reason they had moved.

It is, of course, possible to think about this material in many different ways, but one of the things it seems to me to illustrate is a child's equation of, and confusion at a phantasy level between, the experience of separateness/separation, a connection or link that is damaged or broken, and damage that is the result of the destructive rage of the child (the "storm").

A little over a year into the psychotherapy, the theme of damage crystallised in the transference in a first session after a holiday break, when Isaac was eight years old. Isaac had for some time been using the large square foam cushions in the room to build structures, which kept collapsing.

First session back after a holiday

At the end of the first session after the holiday, I was struck by the way in which Isaac cleaned and tidied the therapy room with uncharacteristic assiduousness and thoroughness which he had never shown before in the therapy (or at home), though in the session he had been no more messy or untidy than usual. I commented to Isaac that he seemed to be taking much more care than usual to clean up and tidy away today. Isaac replied that he had changed. I asked how he had changed, and in response Isaac asked if I had seen a story in the newspaper about a mother of three children who had killed herself. I commented on how awful this was, and then asked why he thought the mother had killed herself; Isaac replied that he thought it might be because she could not cope with her three kids. I pointed out that *his* mother is a mother of three children also, and I suggested he might sometimes worry that he and his brothers were too much for her to cope with. This clearly struck a chord, and Isaac confirmed he did worry about this. I said he might sometimes worry that he causes his mother to feel like the mother in the newspaper story—again Isaac agreed. I then interpreted that he was wanting to make sure today that he did not leave me anything to do at the end, and that I thought he might have a similar worry here that he was "too much" for *me* to cope with and caused *me* to feel like the mother in the newspaper story, and this was the reason for his extra careful cleaning up and tidying away. Isaac said I was right. I linked this anxiety of his with the holiday, and suggested that he might have a thought at the back of his mind that the holiday was because I could not cope with him and needed time away from him.

In this session, I thought Isaac showed an implicit awareness of his mother's depression, and a catastrophic anxiety about being the cause of her state of mind. Two sessions later, Isaac played with a baby tiger figure that he had brought with from home.

Two sessions later

Isaac made the baby tiger bounce excitedly around inside the dolls' house, referring to it as "he" and "him". He said the family are frightened of the tiger because they are worried he might "damage" something. Then the family moved out of the house because of their worry. I took up how the tiger made the family feel and Isaac then constructed two towers beside each other, using the dolls' house furniture, one taller than the other (they were suggestive to me of two figures), which stood where he had put down the family figures in front of the dolls' house. The two towers kept collapsing and he referred to them as "wobbly". I linked these collapsing towers to his previous repeated building of structures with the large square foam cushions, which also kept collapsing. I suggested that what he had made now were like two figures, like a mum and dad, for instance. When I said this, Isaac placed a male figure on the taller "tower" and it fell apart and collapsed. He repeated this several times, rebuilding the towers.

Later, Isaac built a construction with the foam cushions: it consisted of two levels, each with two "legs" and a horizontal section, the overall shape suggesting a body and legs (I did not say this to Isaac).

Isaac got down on the floor and came through the "legs" and emerged out of the front, then patted and climbed on top of the structure, which immediately collapsed. He repeated this several times, trying to rebuild the structure so it would not collapse and fall down. I linked this to the idea of someone who "falls apart" and him being "too much" for them, and to his recent thoughts about a mother who could not cope with her children ... He was pleased when eventually he built a structure that held up under his patting and leaning on it. At the end of the session, when I said there were five more minutes, Isaac suddenly violently smashed the structure down.

Discussion

This material shows the concrete experience and representation of a fragile internal object that is easily "damaged" and collapses "in pieces". It also shows the association and possible confusion between a baby's liveliness on the one hand (the tiger bouncing round the house), and aggression on the other hand (violently smashing down the structure in response to separation at the end of the session), as a cause of damage and of the object's destruction and "falling apart". Over the course of the term, Isaac's preoccupation with being the cause of a damaged and collapsed object/container was elaborated in his play. He repeatedly built enclosed structures with the foam cushions, with himself inside, and every time he emerged the structure collapsed; similarly, he built tunnels with himself inside, and again each time he tried to emerge the tunnel fell apart and collapsed, much to Isaac's frustration. This material evolved during the term into drawings of the *Titanic* and a preoccupation with the catastrophe of its sinking due to the damaged hull and weaknesses in its construction. Isaac had a spontaneous association to the hull of the *Titanic* breaking in two being "like a husband and wife *breaking up*" (my emphasis); what emerged was his anxiety about being the cause of arguments between his parents which he feared might lead to their splitting up (in reality, there was nothing to indicate or suggest the likelihood of parental separation). Here, we see an initial anxiety about a damaged and fragile maternal object segueing into anxiety about a damaged parental couple: the phantasy of damage seems to be carried over from the dyadic to the triadic situation, or from one level of psychic life to another.

Speculatively, I believe there is a link between, on the one hand, the circumstances and experience of Isaac's birth for parents and Isaac, his parents' anxieties after his birth about a damaged baby (no doubt linked to their own damaged objects), mother's probable fragile emotional state during the first two years of Isaac's life, and parents' sense of "something wrong" with Isaac that needed "fixing", and of something "irreparable" in Isaac; on the other hand, Isaac's sense of himself as someone who "break[s] things and can't mend them", his characteristic and pervasive preoccupation in therapy with flimsy or collapsing structures and with causing them to collapse, and his anxiety about being the cause of mother's depression. The common theme running through all these is the damaged object, and the damaging impact of omnipotent thinking associated with a breakdown of differentiation between subject and object.

The damaged object was, thus, a prominent and recurrent theme that constituted a *leitmotif* in the therapy, as in the inner and outer life, of Isaac. The damaged object seemed to operate as a primary (though not exclusive) organiser of mental life, and to have a deterministic influence on "the development of the ego in relation to the external world". The presence of a theme that constitutes a *leitmotif* in a child's (or adult's) psychotherapy is a common phenomenon that will be familiar to any psychoanalyst or psychotherapist.

It seems as if, in non-linear fashion, the initial condition of anxiety about damage to Isaac after his birth exponentially grows in dimension and influence in the minds and inner worlds of Isaac and his parents; over time, it becomes a deterministic non-linear organiser of mental life. In other words, as if the damaged object acts as a strange attractor.

Summary

In this chapter, I have discussed the impact of the damaged object on the development and functioning of psychic life with particular reference to the sense of reality. I have highlighted the importance of the role of external reality in disconfirming phantasies of damage and destruction in the internal world, as emphasised in the theories of Klein and Winnicott. I have elucidated the problem that can arise in psychic functioning and development in a particular constellation of internal and external worlds, where the external world fails to disconfirm, and instead mirrors, phantasies of damage in the internal world, leading to a failure or collapse of the differentiation of internal and external worlds. I have argued that this is different from the confusion or conflation of internal and external worlds, which is a consequence of excessive projective identification.

I have illustrated these themes with a case study in which the damaged object seemed to be a primary organiser of the mental life of a child, and of the clinical material and transference dynamics. In this clinical case, a central preoccupation for the child seemed to be that of damage, and a core unconscious anxiety seemed to be the damaging effect of the child's destructiveness on his objects. For Isaac, the external world failed to disconfirm his ordinary primitive phantasies of damaging his object, and instead an aspect or aspects of his external world (past and present) were felt to mirror or confirm these phantasies.

I have drawn on the scientific concept of the "strange attractor" from chaos theory to characterise the way in which the damaged object can operate as a deterministic influence on psychic life and the relationship to reality when a particular constellation of internal and external worlds occurs.

References

Alvarez, A., & Furgiuele, P. (1997). Speculations on components in the infant's sense of agency: the sense of abundance and the capacity to think in parentheses. In: S. Reid (Ed.), *Developments in Infant Observation* (pp. 123–139). London: Routledge.

Barrows, K. (1999). Ghosts in the swamp: some aspects of splitting and their relationship to parental losses. *International Journal of Psychoanalysis, 80*: 549–561.

Bion, W. R. (1962). *Learning from Experience*. London: Heinemann.

Broucek, F. J. (1979). Efficacy in infancy: a review of some experimental studies and their possible implications for clinical theory. *International Journal of Psychoanalysis, 60*: 311–316.

Broucek, F. J. (1991). *Shame and the Self*. London: Guilford Press.

Bruner, J. (1968). *Processes of Cognitive Growth: Infancy*. Worcester, MA: Clark University Press.

Ferenczi, S. (1913). Stages in the development of the sense of reality. In: *First Contributions to Psycho-Analysis* (pp. 213–239). London: Karnac, 1994.

Freud, S. (1911b). Formulations on the two principles of mental functioning. *S. E., 12*: 218–226. London: Hogarth.

Haag, G. (1985). La mère et le bébé dans les deux moitiés du corps. *Neuropsychiatrie de l'Enfance et de l'Adolescence, 33*: 107–114.

Haag, G. (2000). In the footsteps of Frances Tustin: further reflections on the construction of the body ego. *Journal of Infant Observation, 3*(3): 7–22.

Klein, M. (1930). The importance of symbol-formation in the development of the ego. In: *Love, Guilt and Reparation* (pp. 219–232). London: Hogarth, 1975.

Klein, M. (1932). *The Psychoanalysis of Children*. London: Hogarth.

Klein, M. (1935). A contribution to the psychogenesis of manic-depressive states. In: *Love, Guilt and Reparation* (pp. 262–289). London: Hogarth, 1975.

Klein, M. (1940). Mourning and its relation to manic depressive states. In: *Love, Guilt and Reparation* (pp. 344–369). London: Hogarth, 1975.

Klein, M. (1946). Notes on some schizoid mechanisms. In: *Envy and Gratitude* (pp. 1–24). London: Hogarth, 1975.

Meltzer, D. (1992). *The Claustrum*. Strathtay, Perthshire: Clunie Press.

Papousek, H., & Papousek, M. (1975). Cognitive aspects of preverbal social interaction between human infants and adults. In: R. Porter & M. O'Connor (Eds.), *CIBA Foundation Symposium* (pp. 241–269). Chichester: John Wiley.

Rey, H. (1994). That which patients bring to analysis. In: *Universals of Psychoanalysis in the Treatment of Psychotic and Borderline States* (pp. 229–248). London: Free Association. Originally published in *International Journal of Psychoanalysis, 69*: 457–470.

Rhode, M. (1999). Echo or answer? The move towards ordinary speech in three children with autistic spectrum disorder. In: *Autism and Personality: Findings from the Tavistock Autism Workshop* (pp. 79–92). London: Routledge.

Rhode, M. (2004). Different responses to trauma in two children with autistic spectrum disorder: the mouth as crossroads for the sense of self. *Journal of Child Psychotherapy, 30*(1): 3–20.

Rhode, M. (2005). Mirroring, imitation, identification: the sense of self in relation to the mother's internal world. *Journal of Child Psychotherapy, 31*(1): 52–71.

Rosenfeld, H. (1952). Notes on the psycho-analysis of the super-ego conflict in an acute schizophrenic patient. *International Journal of Psychoanalysis, 33*: 111–131.

Segal, H. (1957). Notes on symbol formation. *International Journal of Psychoanalysis, 38*: 391–397.

Tompkins, S. S. (1981). The quest for primary motives: biography and autobiography of an idea. *Journal of Personality and Social Psychology, 41*: 306–329.

Trevarthen, C., & Hubley, P. (1978). Secondary intersubjectivity: confidence, confiding and acts of meaning in the first year. In: A. Lock (Ed.), *Action, Gesture and Symbol: The Emergence of Language* (pp. 183–229). London: Academic Press.

Tustin, F. (1972). *Autism and Childhood Psychosis*. London: Hogarth.

Tustin, F. (1990). *The Protective Shell in Children and Adults*. London: Karnac.

Winnicott, D. W. (1967). Mirror role of mother and family in child development. In: *Playing and Reality* (pp. 111–118). London: Tavistock, 1971.

Winnicott, D. W. (1971). The use of an object and relating through identifications. In: *Playing and Reality* (pp. 86–94). London: Tavistock.

CHAPTER SIX

The number of sessions per week as an aspect of the psychoanalytical setting: theoretical and technical implications

James Rose

Introduction

The psychoanalytical literature seems to be remarkably silent about the impact of the number of sessions per week on psychoanalytic treatment. It is remarkable because the number of sessions per week is considered by many to be a crucial aspect of the setting. Some seem to have felt that more sessions per week create more impact in a simply additive manner because we can do more given more time. Another way of thinking about impact is to consider the depth of emotional contact that can be achieved by different frequencies of sessions per week. However, if the depth of emotional contact is enhanced by more frequent contact, is this true for all analysands? If it is, are there not some for whom it is emotionally overwhelming? If so, there seems to be a clear case for deepening our understanding of the impact of the frequency of sessions upon the psychoanalytic experience and the particular analysand.

There are a number of implications arising from the lack of a clear reason for distinguishing the effects of increasing frequencies. These include the obvious technical implication of how to recommend to a prospective analysand the frequency appropriate for them. But, there are also wider political implications in that the logic of distinguishing between psychoanalysis, psychotherapy, and counselling on the basis of frequencies per week of treatment comes to appear very arbitrary to the outside world. The result is that it can come to look like arrogance rather than having a sound scientific basis.

What I want to explore in this chapter is a hypothesis that the iterating learning system, implied by the way the psychoanalytic treatment procedure is set up, will, *in and of itself*, disturb psychic defences and, thus, create transference relationships regardless of the content of the interaction between the psychoanalyst and analysand. Thus, the procedure in itself has a therapeutic function quite apart from the work of interpretation. If it can be shown that this may be the case, then does this give us a means of understanding why the number of sessions per week creates the impact we observe it having in our everyday working experience?

How has the effect of the number of sessions per week been thought about?

Quite apart from the political consequences, it does seem to me extraordinary that this essential feature of the psychoanalytical setting has been as neglected, as seems to be the case. In the course of preparing this chapter, I searched the PEP archive for the phrase "number of sessions per week" and turned up some fifty-one references containing that phrase in their text. This seems quite extraordinary, considering the number of references in the archive—some 59,000. Examination of these texts showed that the frequency issue was usually of very marginal relevance to the subject of the text. An exception is a short paper by Gedo and Cohler (1992), who suggested that various factors were concerned in making a judgement about the number of sessions per week necessary or appropriate for any one patient.

In their summary, they argued that

> in most analyses, an increase in frequency will lead to qualitative changes in the data obtained and in the ways each person can use the material. The analysand should generate more associations which focus on the dyadic here and now. Each participant should better understand the other's personalized use of language. More frequent

> sessions should increase the analysand's sense of the "holding environment" and make a deeper therapeutic regression more likely. It should also reduce the analyst's pressure to intervene or introduce "parameters". Efforts to help the analysand deal with his or her shame and acquire missing psychological skills also seem more likely in a maximally intensive therapy. (p. 247)

I think most psychoanalysts would agree with this opinion, although the use of the word "should" implies that the authors recognise that this might not always be the case. However, there is no universally agreed position within those bodies comprising the International Psychoanalytical Association concerning the number of sessions per week required for training purposes. The matter seems to have been largely determined by the particular traditions in any one country arising from the historical development of psychoanalysis in that context. The problem with this situation is that it implies that the psychoanalytic community holds that frequency of sessions per week makes no difference to the psychoanalytical experience and process. Perhaps it has not been much discussed in the literature because the matter is seemingly very controversial.

Freud's views on the matter are reviewed in a paper by Hartocollis (2003): "I work with my patients every day except on Sundays and public holidays – that is, as a rule, six days a week," wrote Freud (1913c, p. 127) in outlining the rules of psychoanalytic technique, which he preferred to call "recommendations" so as not to give the impression that they were unconditional. In fact, for "well advanced" cases, he allowed a reduction to three sessions a week.

Freud (1913c) justified the ideal of daily sessions as follows: "When the hours of work are less frequent, there is a risk of not being able to keep pace with the patient's real life and of the treatment losing contact with the present and being forced into by-paths" (p. 127). Another reason for Freud's insistence on daily sessions was his emphasis on dream analysis and his belief that "the instigating agent of every dream is to be found among the experiences which one has not yet 'slept on'" (1900a, p. 169)—in other words, the day residue of the hours preceding the night of the dream. A related concern had to do with the fact that the temporal distance from the dream event increases the patient's reliance on the word representation and the manifest content of the dream at the expense of the memory of the dream experience as such and its latent content.

In the same paper, Hartocollis refers to Merton Gill's (1984) views thus:

> He (Gill) wrote: It would seem obvious that one can accomplish more with greater frequency simply because there is more time to work. But if greater frequency is frightening to a particular patient, frequent sessions may impede the work despite interpretation. One cannot simply assume that more is better. The optimal frequency may differ from patient to patient. (p. 174)

I find this statement is quite revealing of some assumptions that we can implicitly make about the issue of the frequency of sessions in treatment. If it is "obvious that [we] can accomplish more with greater frequency simply because there is more time to work", we might wonder whether the implicit assumption is that the impact of increasing sessions occurs in an arithmetically additive manner. If others are frightened by an increase in frequency, why should this be? It leaves a question: if it is to be the responsibility of the psychoanalyst to "gauge the dose", then what criteria should be borne in mind to optimise the efficacy of the treatment? Should these criteria be solely concerned with the nature of the analysand? Or should we think about the characteristics of the psychoanalytic procedure itself? Another question would be what difference is created in the psychoanalytical experience as a result of increasing the number of sessions per week. If the increase in impact is simply additive, this does not account for why many psychoanalysts seem to agree that there is a qualitative change in the psychoanalytical experience as the number of sessions per week increases (see Gedo & Cohler, 1992, above, and Etchegoyen, 1992, below).

Two other factors that have been, perhaps cynically, mentioned as having a bearing on what ultimately becomes the frequency of treatment in any one case have been identified as the fee and/or other, what might be thought to be, practicalities or exigencies, for example, geographical distances. Various commentators (e.g., Quinodoz, 1992) have observed that this can be a reflection of the treating psychoanalyst's countertransference to the patient. To this might be cynically added the treating psychoanalyst's expectations about the level of financial income they hope to gain from their efforts compared with the analysand's desire for treatment and ability to pay.

The psychoanalytic process considered
as an iterative learning system

When we commence a treatment, we create a system that has the task of learning something about the analysand's psychic reality. It can be readily assumed that this is a system comprising ourselves as a psychoanalyst and the analysand meeting in a setting that to the outsider seems to vary as little as possible.

Spatially, the setting can be said to be a consulting room that remains essentially unchanged throughout the treatment. Temporally, the frequency of meetings per week is agreed at the outset and this might, or might not, remain unchanged throughout the course of the treatment. What does change will arise partly from the result of the learning of the first session feeding forward into the next one. Again, this continues throughout the treatment and it is this feature that makes it possible to think of the system as an iterative one.

Calling the psychoanalytical learning system iterative might seem simply descriptive, but I use it intentionally because I propose that it enables us to bring some conceptual tools to bear that are derived from the theory of complex, dynamic systems. There are two characteristic features of iterative systems: repetition determined by an algorithm (a procedure or set of rules for calculation) and feedback. They are called iterative systems because they repeatedly take something in, transform it in some way, and export the results. These results then become the input back into the system, and transformation and export repeats in an iterating cycle. In psychoanalysis, this cyclical and iterating feature creates a situation in which patterns of a person's feelings and behaviour that essentially control their lives can be accurately discerned in the minutiae of everyday life—one might call it the daily life of the transference relationship in an analysis. Some psychoanalysts have been thinking, in relatively recent years, about the application of ideas about complex, dynamic systems to understanding psychoanalytic process: for example, Galatzer-Levy (1995, 2009); Moran (1991); Piers (2000, 2005); Quinodoz (1997).

Galatzer-Levy (1995), for example, has shown that samples of psychoanalytic material from any one patient commonly have strikingly self-similar aspects. Here is an example that he took from the analysis of an obsessional patient, looked at on what he called several levels of magnification. Thus, he looked at material brought by a patient from a perspective of looking at the patterns of feeling and experience over a period of a year to what might be called the "here and now". Reading this material may well give the feeling that year-long magnification is like reading a case history, whereas the shorter time scale magnifications come to feel increasingly like reading process notes. Hence, we can experience the intense affect contained in descriptions of process material. All will no doubt agree that it is from this affect that the mutative quality of the psychoanalytical experience largely derives because it emerges in the context of the transference relationship.

Year-long magnification

Mr A first exhibited obsessional symptoms at age seven, following his mother's remarriage. To others he seemed withdrawn, but in fact his time was spent fretfully counting objects in his room and worrying that something was missing. His symptoms were relieved by psychotherapy. Although he remained inhibited and rather meticulous, he did fairly well until he was eleven. Then, apparently in response to puberty and tension in his mother's marriage, he again became symptomatic. He worried that he had not completed homework assignments and was so concerned to eat properly that charting the nutritional values of food disrupted his life. There were other less prominent obsessional symptoms. The patient interrupted a second round of psychotherapy by a conscious decision to suppress obsessional symptoms, which he did until he left home to go to college. In the uncontrolled, sexually liberal atmosphere of the college dormitory, Mr A became anxious and severely obsessional, worried that the cafeteria food might be bad for him, that he had prepared for his class inadequately, and that he was dressed improperly.

Months-long magnification

Mr A wanted very much to "do it (the analysis) right". In part based on his past therapeutic experience, he approached analysis by expressing jarringly intense feelings. Both the patient and the analyst regarded these expressions as deeply authentic and representative of major analytic progress. Often, after several weeks of talking in this way, the affect intensified further. At these times, the patient demanded the analyst's direct assistance in managing the affects and, partly because the analyst did not know how to help him, became increasingly anxious. He feared going mad. This sense lasted for at most a couple of days. Then the patient regularly first became angry with the analyst for failing to manage some aspect of the analysis correctly (such as billing for missed sessions), and subsequently became enmeshed in sorting out the failing (e.g., developing elaborate moral arguments for and against charging for missed sessions).

Analytic hours

Mr A began most analytic sessions with some topic in mind about which he felt strongly. He developed it at some length. (For example, he would speak with rage about his father's departure.) After the topic had been engaged, the analyst often made a defence interpretation. (The analyst agreed that the patient was angry with his father for leaving but wondered whether his more immediate anger was not addressed to the analyst, who had recently returned from vacation.) At first, the patient engaged the interpretation vigorously. ("You always think it's you. You, you, you! But you don't think it's you enough not to go on your stupid vacations!") Then the patient began a much less affective, more intellectual discussion of why he had used the identified defence. ("I wonder why I use displacement so much. That is the right term, isn't it?") As the session drew to a close, the patient often felt it was urgent that he finish the discussion before the session's end. Frequently, he tried to get out a few more sentences as he left. The analyst encouraged him to leave and assured him that the topic could be addressed more fully in the next session.

Analytic minutes

Attending closely to the patient's speech revealed that it was marked by constant interruptions, either as dysfluencies or interrupting self-reference.

"I hate my er father because he uh he uh he uh he kinda doesn't, I mean didn't. I find this hard to say. He didn't uh do uh. He didn't do what sorta what er he needed to do for me. Pause. You're going to ask what that was. Well he didn't uh do it! I can't describe it. You know! He kinda didn't! (Galatzer-Levy, 1995, p. 1108)

Galatzer-Levy commented, "The obsessional phenomena described here are familiar to all analysts. No one of them is more essential than another. They can all be seen as aspects of the same self-similar structure view with differing temporal magnification" (p. 1108).

The impact on this patient of his father's disappearance and its effect upon his psychic reality and functioning can be readily observed. He seems haunted by an absence of something important to him, which is projected to his possessions and the world around him. He seeks to defend against a terrible resulting anxiety by reassuring himself that it is not, in fact, missing or by being sure that whatever he puts into the empty absence inside him will be healthy and nourishing. This very possibly shows us that he experienced this internal emptiness as painfully toxic. His understanding of close relationships being constantly in the shadow of imminent abandonment readily shows a deep anxiety requiring a variety of defences to hold himself together. With the intensity of the patient's attachment to his object increasing with increasing numbers of sessions per week, we can expect that the patient will experience week-ends and other breaks very keenly.

All psychoanalysts know that it is through the psychoanalyst interpretatively linking the patients' experience of themselves and their analyst in the context of the psychoanalytic setting that enables a patient to come to understand how and why he experiences as he does. Experience arises from our impulses, the anxiety that might be aroused by these impulses, and the defences we create against these anxieties. We can see in the above material that as the time-scale of magnification becomes shorter, the analysand's affect becomes more apparent as the "here and now" is approached. This is doubtless a result of the strengthening attachment of the analysand to his analyst. As dependency increases, so does the feeling aroused by the absence of the object in the transference. It is these feelings that must be experienced in order to create the impetus for change and make it possible. As the experience of these feelings becomes more conscious, there will be a threat of overwhelming anxiety and an opportunity, as a result, to see how various defences, created to contain the anxiety, function, yet, possibly amplify it, because they are ineffective. With this material, Galatzer-Levy vividly shows how an analyst and their analysand may develop a cognitive understanding of the analysand's problems. However, the stuff of psychic change springs from the affects of experience.

The strange attractor observed in clinical material

This clinical material was given by Galatzer-Levy as an example of how a structure of clinical material replicates itself in the course of psychoanalytical treatment. This feature will be familiar to all practising psychoanalysts. This repetition of structure is an indication of something that partly determines the manifest behaviour of iterative systems. This something is referred to in the theory of iterative systems as a strange attractor, which has been described above. (See Chapter One.) In the case of the patient just reviewed, the strange attractor seems to be the haunting absent figure of the father. It draws attention to itself by the massive efforts to defend against the anxieties it arouses, which are directly affecting the patient's behaviour. But, while the strange nature of this behaviour is obvious to others, it might seem less so to the patient because it has become part of his anguished existence and daily experience. In effect, the patient will very probably be unconscious of these patterns and, thus, unable to reflect upon them.

The notion of the strange attractor was introduced and described in Chapter One. It is a concept that comes closer to putting the idea of an internal object or an unconscious phantasy into mathematical terms than anything else I have encountered. Those psychoanalysts referred to above with an interest in the application of the theory of complex non-linear dynamic systems to an understanding of the mind all refer to the concept. This is because the concept helps us to conceptualise in logical terms the everyday experience in psychoanalytic work in which psychoanalysts find themselves being dynamically pulled in various directions and into different situations by the presence of what are clearly psychic phenomena. These could be thought of as internal objects and their associated drives and defences.

Over a period of time, one can discern common and repeating patterns of behaviour and feeling, which reflect themes that have an obvious relevance to the reasons that brought the analysand to his analysis (as seen in Galatzer-Levy's example of clinical experience given above). Of course, this is reflected in the *conscious* psychic content of the material, but what strikes me, often in the counter-transference, is the insistent presence of a something that lurks on the edge of conscious experience. It is insistent in the sense that it seems to be highly influential and draws attention to itself, but it seems sometimes very reluctant to allow itself to be contemplated in reflective consciousness. We can also observe episodes in an analysis where the flow of associations seems to stop, be diverted, and there is a change in the analytic atmosphere in the consulting room. Often, there seems to be an implicit threat that, if it is allowed to enter reflective consciousness, there will be a breakdown into chaos. We can see in the clinical material above, descriptive of analytic minutes, that there seems to be a sense that the analyst is being told he is not doing something but that this is very frightening for the analysand to contemplate telling him directly, perhaps for fear of a further rejection. This leads to the defensive displacement of affect from the psychoanalyst to the father, which, in turn, places the psychoanalyst in the position of being a disregarded, or assumed, third. As discussed above, the absence of something important to him seems to have haunted the analysand and created the patterns of affect and cathect that dominate him. Without the concept that this haunting entity is in his mind, these behavioural patterns might seem beyond reason to those around him—indeed mad. Clinically, for example, phenomena like this often will be clearly observed in the treatment of depressed patients suffering from unconscious guilt. As the cause of the guilt approaches consciousness, the patient might become very anxious and fearful of breakdown.

As discussed in Chapter One, the idea of a strange attractor comes from the theory of iterating systems. It refers to a pattern of cyclical dynamic motion towards which such a system tends. It comes from the observation that consistent patterns can be observed in the behaviour of iterative systems over a period of time even though they might appear at any one moment to be behaving randomly. They are seemingly "attracted" towards these patterns even if, once within them, they might seem to be randomly determined. As these observations accumulate, it is possible to discern something that determines these patterns of behaviour. Jean-Michel Quinodoz (1999) pointed out that Jacques Ruelle, the originator of the "strange attractor" concept, himself referred to his term as "psychoanalytically suggestive". Perhaps this is because the term strange attractor sounds like a thing, whereas it is a term to describe a pattern. It can be applied, therefore, to understand a pattern of behaviour or, indeed, affect. In psychoanalysis, it could be thought of as referring to the patterns of affect that can be observed in the transference and countertransference interaction.

In essence, my argument is that the possibility of the observation and identification of strange attractors in psychic reality arises out of the continued iteration of the encounter between analysand and his psychoanalyst. As we could see in the clinical material above, consistencies of structure, when seen, arise from the repeated observation of the analysand over a period of time. This is because we have to have a context of repeated observations of patterns in which to see the significance of the "here and now". On early encounter with any one patient, we might be able to form hypotheses concerning the reasons for that patient's need for an analysis. However, until we have had the opportunity to observe the patient over a period of time, all we will be doing is superimposing our understanding on the situation. This is inevitable initially, but all psychoanalysts will know that these initial impressions must be open to question in the light of our ongoing experience of an analysis.

There is no attempt yet to show how learning might occur. However, if we postulate that all learning systems display features common to iterative systems, that is, iterating intake, transformation of intake, and output feeding back into the system, then understanding some features of these systems has a clear relevance for psychoanalytic practice. My intention here is to offer some thoughts on how our understanding of the workings of the psychoanalytic learning system can be enhanced if we consider what has been found about iterative systems, not just in the empirical sense, but also what is to be expected about how *any such* system will function.

In the broadest of outline, we can say that the task of the psychoanalyst is to offer observations and interpretations on the ongoing process between the psychoanalyst and analysand in the light of the situation as it unfolds between them. With these observations, the psychoanalyst and the analysand might be able to make links between how the analysand experiences the here-and-now, his past, and his future. These links will arise from the psychoanalyst's experience: that is, her feelings and her conscious reflections on these feelings. Through working in this way with the analysand, the defences developed in his past life will become observable and, thereby, implicitly or explicitly challenged. These defences will be manifest in the observable patterns of emotion in the psychoanalytic process.

This is the stuff of psychoanalytic learning and is never simply cognitive, but potentially saturated with affect. With this comes the possibility of change because the defences, created by the patient to deal with difficult experiences, are gradually revealed to be ineffective. Yet, there is no avoiding these experiences in the process of change. With this confrontation comes the threat of the possibility of chaos as the defences threaten to collapse and anxiety is aroused. But the experience of the defences against these anxieties provide the impetus to change, as these defences are revealed to be ineffective or, indeed, are partly responsible for creating the anxieties against which they are supposed to defend.

Thus, it is bound to be a disturbing experience and, if the patient is not to take flight, this disturbance and the consequent anxiety will have to be, in some way, managed or contained. As Galatzer-Levy (2009) recently put it,

> A general principle of non-linear dynamics is that complexity emerges on the edge of chaos (Langston, 1990). For a system to have rich multiple possibilities involves it being nearly chaotic and at risk of falling into chaos. If one of the goals of analysis is developing a capacity for a richer, more complex way of dealing with psychological events, this principle implies that hoped for psychic change risks disorganization. There is an inevitable compromise between stability, the need for novelty, and the risk of chaos. The sense that new ideas are dangerous and that development often risks trauma is a central dilemma, not only for analysands, but for all people who are changing. Ideally one explores novelty as freely as possible without risking disorganization. (p. 987)

What Galatzer-Levy is indicating is that iterative systems not only reveal their structure through the emergence of strange attractors, but also have the property of being morpho-genetic. In other words, they create and develop their structure as a reaction to the conditions in which they find themselves. In so doing, they can seem to "learn". This property has very obvious relevance because it suggests that the psychoanalytic procedure itself promotes this development quite apart from the content of what goes on between the psychoanalyst and the analysand.

There is nothing, I would contend, that is controversial in what I have said. However, the question I wish to explore is whether the observable patterns in the clinical material are partly the product of the iterating learning system that, *in and of itself*, will do this regardless of the actual content of the intercourse between the psychoanalyst and the analysand. What follows from this question is whether increasing the number of sessions per week will make this more possible.

Contemporary theorists of dynamic iterative systems would, as I understand them, contend that this is bound to be observed. This is because, by observing the results of iteration over time, the strange attractors of all such systems can be observed. In certain situations something chaotic emerges, which might sound rather frightening, but what this means is that readily understood and predictable relationships between variables, which might be expected to be described by (line)ar equations[1] give way to a situation in which one cannot predict *output y* from *input x* using such equations. In other words, one has to understand something about the transformative system to understand why output occurs in the way it does. It occurs even if the procedure governing the iteration is entirely deterministic. Indeed, in some situations (as we shall see later), there can be many possible values of *output y*, all equally valid. In these situations, chaos is said to ensue and the system under study is often said to be non-linear. This can sound rather mystical, but what it means is that the system cannot be modelled mathematically by straightforward linear equations as above. It also means that the internal workings of the system in question are not readily and immediately understandable.

I propose, therefore, that disturbance necessary for change and development occurs *partly* as a result of the kind of treatment setting, one feature of which is the number of sessions per week, within which the psychoanalyst and the analysand work. Now, how can I make such a proposal? To do so, I shall try to describe some ideas about iterating systems. These systems need not necessarily be learning systems but I shall contend that the principles remain the same because of the iterative nature of the psychoanalytical procedure. Further, as indicated above, it can, with justification, be said that all learning systems are iterative in nature.

To do this we need to look in some detail at an example of an iterating system, which is more complex than a pendulum, as discussed in Chapter One. Let us begin by looking at some strange phenomena concerning the growth and decline of populations of animals, insects, or birds. Observation, year on year, will show that the numbers of any one population are not easily predictable without knowing about the age of the population and its death rate, the abundance of the food supply, and other possibly random variations in environmental conditions. What is observed, over a period of years, is that while it is difficult to predict exactly the size of the population, year on year, numbers will settle into a range of values between extinction and exponential growth. These ranges of values can be thought of as manifesting strange attractors because they become characteristic unless there is some major change in the food supply. This is because the size of the population is determined by the birth rate and the death rate, which is proportional to the birth rate.

A population of a particular species in a particular environment can, therefore, be thought of as a complex iterative system. It has evolved in this way because the gene pool that it manifests has found a way of reproducing itself in such a way that takes account of the effect of environmental fluctuation in the short or long term. The unpredictability built into the reproductive process allows the flexibility necessary for successful evolution and has survival value for the gene pool. This might seem a long way from an understanding of the mind, yet, if the mind is a part of a system (a human being) that must be responsive to its environment in order to survive, then the analogy seems to me to become more direct.

In taking this example, the reader might well ask what relevance this has for understanding the psychoanalytic learning system. The point is that it makes possible a *mathematical abstraction*. This is not done to put a mathematical veneer on the psychoanalytic process, but to open up a number of questions.

1.   By using a mathematical model governing iterative systems, does it become possible to write equations that show the relationship between variables that are otherwise hard to link?

2. Can we use the mathematical abstraction to think about why increasing the number of weekly iterations of the psychoanalytic learning system will create patterns of experience?

3. Can we use the mathematical model to conceptualise how different aspects of the analysand have a bearing on the impact of the psychoanalytic procedure, which might help us when we are assessing the analysand at the outset and deciding the optimal treatment?

To begin to explore the workings of complex iterative systems further, let us imagine an island; and on that island, there is a population of animals numbering Ny in year y. The capacity for this species' population to increase numerically in the next year (y +1) will vary according to its *fertility and the capacity of the environment* to support the increased population. It will also be affected by *mortality*—expressed as a function of the numbers of individuals surviving in year y.

This can be expressed mathematically as: $N_{(y + 1)} = N_y (a - bN_y)$ which is known as the *logistic equation*, where N_y is the number in the population in year y and $N_{(y+1)}$ is the population the following year and is the sum of those alive following reproduction less those who have died.

Where a is a constant expressing the reproductive efficiency of the species. If breeding were unrestrained and there were no death of some of the population, population growth would be defined by the equation $N y+1 = a.N y$ and we would observe exponential growth.

In reality, population growth is limited by food supply and other competitive factors, so we would want to add a term to the above equation to allow for this, which will reduce the numbers actually observed. As we are observing a population on an island, that is, a limited space, the food supply will be finite and, hence, we can say that the greater the population, the less food there will be for each individual. We can say, as an approximation, that the *probability of death for each individual* is proportional to the total population; we may say that the actual death rate for the population *as a whole* is proportional to Ny^2; say $b.Ny^2$, where b is another constant expressing the chances of death in any one year *of an individual member*. The *actual number* dying will, therefore, will be proportional to the number of the population.

If we want to follow the growth or decline of the population over a period of years, we can use the equation above in an iterating manner. We can then calculate what the population could be expected to be from year y_1 to year y_{n+x} over whatever time scale (n + x years) in which we were interested. We can also predict whether the population could be expected to grow or decline to extinction. Thus, the logistic equation is the mathematical expression of an iterating algorithm. As we can see, growth, decline, or stabilisation is partly determined by α, but not in a simple additive way. This is because the death rate, which results from the finite food supply on an island, is proportional to the numbers in the previous year. Thus, the population number is determined by two countervailing variables, which are not independent of one another.

What this means is that, while we can say what values of a predict the population's decline to extinction, we will also observe those values of a that lead to a growth, to a stability such that birth rate is balanced by death rate. But, while we can predict growth and extinction, what we cannot do is to predict year on year precisely what the population numbers will be because a will not remain constant. Hence, we can see the difficulty of trying to predict precisely a system made complex by the countervailing forces that are not independent of each other.

How might this apply to an understanding of the psychoanalytic procedure?

Let us start with the perhaps unusual, but not, I think, particularly contentious, idea that the psychoanalytic procedure can be defined as an iterative learning system. If it is iterative then the product of a session (n) must feed forward in some way into session (n+1). If it is thus iterative, then it will follow the same principles governing all iterative systems. After all, why should it be any different? Some might reply that the difference is that two complex systems are interacting with each other. However, in this paper, we are studying the impact on the analysand of variations in the psychoanalytical setting. Furthermore, while it is true that two complex systems are working with one another, the psychoanalyst is trained in the use of the procedure to be as constant and stabilising as possible in so far as their role is defined by the setting. They vary, of course, in their work of inter-pretation, in so far as they respond to the analysand. Moreover, no two psychoanalysts will be identical in how they respond to the analysand.

It might be hard to see how we can define α in the psychoanalytic iterative system, conceptually defined by a logistic equation of the form

$$N(y + 1) = Ny(a - bNy),$$

with which we are familiar from above, but it is not impossible to imagine it.

In broad terms, we might say that a represents those factors which are to do with growth, linking, and opening relationships with those outside the individual and with the environment. Thus, we might take a to indicate the capacity of the system to increase learning (a kind of psychic fertility). There will be an incentive to do this because of the greater chances of survival in the psychic sense.

This comprises the willingness of the analysand to learn; but a will also be effected by the frequency of meeting if this increases the ease with which the patterns of affect can be observed in the immediacy of contact between psychoanalyst and analysand and their replication over lengthening periods of time. This is because the experience of these observations is what feeds forward into the next session, which enables the conflict of contact and separation to arise with sufficient strength.

With increasing dependence on the analyst, the patterns of affect will become more observable and vividly experienced by both the analyst and the analysand. Thus, we saw above how the structure of affect in a patient's psychic reality became more apparent in the minute by minute (or "here and now") in a manner that reflected a perspective gained from looking at his developmental history over his lifetime and the course of the treatment. However, the immediacy of everyday contact seems to enable the emotional impact or consequen-ces of the analysand's psychic structures to be experienced by both analysand and the psychoanalyst within themselves and between their complementary roles.

One is reminded of Freud's preference for seeing a patient daily. Thus, his insistence on daily sessions derived from his emphasis on dream analysis and his belief that "the instigating agent of every dream is to be found among the experiences which one has not yet 'slept on'" (1900a, p. 169)—in other words, the day residue of the hours preceding the night of the dream. A related concern had to do with the fact that the temporal distance from the dream event increases the patient's reliance on the word representation and the manifest content of the dream at the expense of the memory of the dream experience as such and its latent content. The feeling of the dream is lost and replaced by a memory narrative based on words. The rawness of affect, thus, is replaced by cognitive secondary revision and an essential aspect of the learning experience is lost. The result is that the opportunity for free association to the dream material is impeded.

On the other hand, b could represent all those factors that are to do with breaking links and relationships both within the individual and between him/her and the outside world. Thus, b could be taken to represent resistance and partly be a function of learning that has occurred in sessions up to Ln. Resistance is essentially resistance to change because change creates anxiety. In plainer words, b corresponds to the emotional impact of the cognitive and emotional learning represented by a.

For example, a negative therapeutic reaction is a clear reaction to learning in preceding sessions. Another example of how it may be observed *in extremis* is Britton's (2004) conception of what he called psychic atopia, which might be thought of as a tendency to avoid other minds or even the thought that one has a mind of one's own. In this case, b is a function of the analysand's psychic structure and the functioning of that structure.

The parallels with open systems theory models (Von Bertalanffy, 1950) thus become very clear. The analysand, as an open system, must be in interaction with his environment—if only simply to stay alive—and must, at the same time, defend himself by maintaining his boundaries. Furthermore, open systems are iterative systems because they are in continual interaction with their environment.

Thus, a tentative conceptual stab at a logistic equation describing a psychoanalytic learning system might be

$$Ln+1 = Ln(a - bLn)$$

Put in more vernacular terms: the amount of learning in any one session equals (or, possibly more accurately, is a function of) the amount of learning in the preceding session less the reduction due to resistance.

The crucial point is that this equation is the same in structure as the logistical equation outlined above. Hence, it can be expected that, on the basis of what we have seen above, that there are circumstances in which the system it models will become chaotic in the sense that predictable linearities will start to become unpredictable.

In other words, we can predict that the psychoanalytic learning system *has the potential to become chaotic (or unpredictable)* because of its iterative nature. However, we may also propose that it is this feature that gives it its power. As the number of sessions increases then so does L (learning). This is because the iterating nature of the psycho-analytical learning system will start to reveal the strange attractors governing the analysand's psychic life. However, the anxiety thus stirred by the possibility of change, as represented by b, will impede the growth of L (learning) to the point possibly of overwhelming it. This will be observed in the ongoing psychoanalytical process and be revealed by characteristic patterns of behaviour, feeling, and experience in the transference and the countertransference. It also predicts the possibility of impasse when the anxiety implied by learning overwhelms the increase of learning.

We must here note that we cannot yet, in this case, insert interval data (or numbers which can used for arithmetical computation) into this equation as we can when thinking about population growth or decline. However, what we can do is say that Learning can increase but this will not be additive because resistance can increase in a manner proportional to that Learning. Thus, we can propose that learning will increase but we cannot say by how much because we are using ordinal data (see Siegel, 1956); thus, while we can say that 2 is greater than 1, we cannot say that 2 is twice 1.

This will make intuitive sense to a psychoanalyst. While we cannot yet meaningfully quantify learning in the arithmetical sense, we can justifiably observe that learning has increased. We can observe that the analysand begins to bear and stay in touch with intense feelings and she increasingly reflects and sees herself in relation to others. We can also know when an analysand has become stuck in the sense that potential learning is being negated by resistance. Moreover, we can go a step further in our use of these conceptual models of the psycho-analytic process.

This is because the process has the potential over time to reveal the analysand's patterns of affect manifest in the emergence of strange attractors functioning in the immediacy of the session and the overall process of the analysis, as we saw above in Galatzer-Levy's clinical material. Accompanying these revelations will be the observation of the analysand's customary resistances, which prevent the patterns of affect becoming conscious and, thus, impede learning. If the psychoanalyst does not prevent this by imposing their understanding prematurely, the functioning of the analysand's psychic reality will be replicated in the emerging transference relationship.

Finding an effective balance of these two tendencies (*a* and *b*) helps us define what we mean by managing the potential of the psychoanalytical procedure both to disturb the analysand—and, thus, promote change—and to contain the anxiety that will be the inevitable consequence of psychic change. However, we cannot ignore the fact that the crucial determinant of the onset of chaos in the demonstration above was the variable *a*. If *a* is too small in respect of *b*, then no learning can occur. In other words, it partly concerns something to do with the setting in which learning takes place. The point of using this simple mathematical model is to study the effect of increasing frequency of treatment and whether its effect can be expected to be additive in a linear manner, or to follow some other form. We must conclude the latter.

Using this rather rough and ready conceptual model, we can then predict that the greater the opportunity for the patient to express himself and to allow the analyst (and the patient) to make observations of the patient, the easier it will be to reveal relatively stable and consistent manifestations of unconscious mental processes. However, the patient's resistances are also greater in proportion to the degree of what has been learned. In terms of the analysand's experience, he will find himself unconsciously presented with choices about how to experience the situation and his psychoanalyst within it. Becoming conscious of these choices will reveal characteristic patterns of engagement with others in his psychic and external worlds that, however unsuccessful, have been built up over many years. It might be expected that it would be a relief if he changes these patterns, but experience shows that it might also be threatening and, thus, resistance occurs.

This resistance will seemingly diminish the efficacy of the learning process, but is inevitable. So a paradoxical situation obtains: the greater the frequency, the more successful the learning. However, the more successful the learning, the more intense the resistances and, thus, the less learning seems to take place. The result is that more frequent sessions will tend to influence the resistances in a complex (non-linearly additive) manner. This is due to the resistive reaction to the greater degree of learning. That learning is also being hampered and diminished in quantitative proportion to the frequency of sessions, regardless of the degree of learning. Against this, we must balance the fact that observing resistances is part of the learning. Nevertheless, we must expect that the analysand *might respond* to the psychoanalytic process by creating a defensive organisation that effectively seeks to negate any learning. This is a powerful defence, which is probably reflected in his life, but which, none the less, is there to be observed. It could be what brought him into an analysis.

Accordingly, with greater frequency of sessions, complex changes will take place in the resistances and, therefore, in the learning that takes place. If that learning is progressive in a positive direction, our model predicts that, at a critical point, the patient's stable psychic structure will become destabilised and unanticipated, unpredicted, and unpredictable phenomena will ensue in the manifest clinical picture. This stage, conceived here solely as a result of greater frequency, will give both participants an opportunity to observe and learn about very important psychic aspects of the patient that were not previously manifest.

To be sure, we might see, at this critical point, that the resistances of the patient overwhelm the motivation to learn; and the learning process may well be impeded by the development of a defensive organisation against the analytic process itself. Nevertheless, observation of such a development can potentially tell us a great deal about how an analysand manages the dynamics of his psychic life when demands are placed upon him/her to change or adapt. However, where these defensive manoeuvres and resistances can be observed and, from this, managed through interpretations and other interventions, the opportunity thus produced has the potential to be mutative. It is mutative in a manner quite unlike that seen in other forms of psychotherapy of lesser frequencies because it is far more dynamic. This is because the interaction of learning and resistance are much easier to observe for both analyst and analysand.

The conceptual model also predicts that, after this critical development in the patient's clinical condition takes place, the patient's destabilised psychic structure will tend to fluctuate within a relatively narrow range, which is defined by the effects of the learning that has been achieved. This is because of the increasing effect of resistance. The concomitant effect is that the resistances that have been organised in accordance to the learning that has been achieved can be observed. In accordance with the greater frequency, the resistances have a correspondingly greater potential to be revealed within a narrow range of fluctuation. Within this narrow range of fluctuation much exploratory and interpretative work can be accomplished due to its quasi-stable/unstable properties. We might say that this could provide a transitional space (following Winnicott's formulation) in which to play and contemplate new patterns of psychic life.

Some thoughts on making recommendations to potential analysands on frequency of treatment

In making assessments of potential analysands and recommendations for their treatment, we have to balance various factors in terms of the impact that they are likely to have on effective treatment. What it is that has led them to contemplate embarking on an analysis can range from a feeling that life is impossible without help to an intellectual curiosity about the workings of their mind. Or, it might be because they wish to embark on training as a psychoanalyst. This wish is very likely to be over-determined, of which we will have to take account: for example, are they seeking to avoid being an analysand?

We will pay attention not only to what they say about themselves, but also to how they appear to respond to the assessment experience and what they arouse in our countertransference. Through this, we will derive a preliminary formulation of the manner of their psychic functioning, which has led to their approach for help. We will get a sense of the urgency of their need for help, the origins of their disturbance, a sense of their characteristic defences expressed in their statements and enactments, and a sense of the fundamental integrity of their psychic functioning.

If we return to Galatzer-Levy's rubric for structuring his clinical material, above, we might say that, in assessment, we get a partial year-long magnification view which is very largely cognitive in its quality. We will probably get a better feel for the manner in which this is experienced by the potential analysand if we choose to have several assessment sessions. Then, in making recommendations concerning frequency, we have to balance how far the analysand is bringing problems stemming from the fundamental building blocks of the self, for example, fundamental attachment issues, or whether the problems concern transitions and losses in the context of a well-functioning personality.

Next, we have to think about how this individual might react to the psychoanalytic learning system. We can make, at best, estimations about how he will experience its impact. For some, having frequent sessions will be an enormous relief; for others, the prospect of it could be very threatening. I suggest that, in practice, we balance the severity of the difficulties that the patient brings against the difficulties and the distastes that the patient is likely to experience once treatment has begun. The patient is likely to face feelings stirred in the transference, which are uncomfortable and frightening to her because her defences are challenged. This can be aroused by her resistance to change and also by the depth of the regression which is brought about by her dependency on her psychoanalyst. The typical practice in the treatment of adolescents is to have a lower frequency because they are often afraid of becoming dependent. What a patient cannot foresee are his own reactions when those periods occur in which his characteristic defences begin to be examined.

On the other hand, as psychoanalysts, we can predict that these periods are bound to occur because of our professional knowledge of the process. A patient cannot foresee this, but psychoanalysts are in a position to know that this will happen and will evoke considerable anxiety in our patients. We have to take this into account and find a balance between the necessity of disturbing the defences and containing the anxieties that will be inevitably aroused.

For me, the value of the conceptual model has been to help me make assessments for treatment in a more systematic way and, especially, to regard the impact of the setting and the number of sessions planned per week as having, *in itself*, a bearing upon the treatment. Further, it is the beginning of a model that brings together the characteristics of the analysand and the impact of the setting. Absence of consideration of this matter in the literature seems to me to suggest that very often we simply begin and see what happens. This is indicative that we have tended to take the setting for granted. This is in spite of the fact that we know that a psychoanalytic process cannot take place outside a setting.

What can be gained from thinking about the psychoanalytic procedure as an iterative learning system?

When we think about the effect of increasing the number of sessions per week, we might generally expect that potentially learning would increase. But, in individual cases, what we cannot predict is how it increases and neither can we predict the impact of the analysand's resistance to learning. Thus, I think we can say that the effect or impact of four sessions per week for any one patient is potentially likely to be greater than two. Moreover, in assessing a potential analysand, we have to balance the relative strength of variables a and b. As the treatment begins and is in process, we will observe that learning and resistance are in dynamic interaction so that each entails the other.

At this point, it is important to keep in mind that we are looking at the logic of the structure of an iterative learning system. There is the question that this is all very well but, unless the variables a and b can be objectively measured using data enabling arithmetical computations to be made, it is hard to see how the model can be developed. However, I think we can state that that the effect, or impact, of four sessions per week for any one patient is likely to be greater than two, but what we cannot say is that the impact will be *twice as great in the arithmetic sense*. Provided we are clear about this, we can satisfactorily and validly study the logic of the system using the model derived from the logistic equation.

Empirical data that has a bearing on this question can be gained from Fonagy and Target's (1996) retrospective study of treatments carried out at the Anna Freud Centre. The interesting finding that children younger than twelve do better when treated intensively and tend to be more likely to terminate prematurely when they are treated less intensively, is perhaps counter-intuitive to most adult minds.

We might wonder whether such children are in the process of "learning to stand on their own feet". Thus, they look for a stronger adult presence to help them because they feel more dependent. In contrast, the finding that adolescents do better when treated less intensively makes more sense when we consider that these are individuals who are in a process of growing to achieve individuality and for whom dependency can seem subversive to that process. Thus, we see here the interaction between learning and resistance working in different ways depending on the nature of the analysand.

Do we need the mathematical model to understand this feature? In making the observations alone, probably not, but the model does help to make explicit the relationship between learning and resistance in understanding the empirical result above. The implication is that, in assessment, we need to think about how the potential analysand, of whatever age, will react to a learning process. We might think of this as how they will behave in, and react to, an analysis. This has implications for training in effective assessment. Effectively, the question becomes: given what we know of what has brought the analysand for treatment and what our impression is of the nature and development of his psychic structure, what frequency of treatment will optimally promote learning while taking account of whether he might respond to that learning by developing a defensive organisation that could obviate any potential to learn?

We must also take into account that it is customary to gear the number of times a patient is seen to a weekly cycle. We think of sessions per week and not a month or a year. Thus, there are implicitly two patterns of iteration: a weekly cycle and then the number of sessions per week. We can use the conceptual model to study the effects upon output. This shows us that the effect of increasing numbers of sessions will not be linear or additive. Because of the qualitative change in the experience of increasing numbers of sessions per week and because the effect on output can be shown to be determined by a non-linear or parabolic model, we must conclude that potentially any one analysand will react to the setting in a manner independent of whatever emerges in the content of the analysis.

However, the implication of this is that, while we can conceptually separate out the characteristics of different frequencies of iteration for the iterative learning system, we have to distinguish this from the impact these different frequencies of treatment will have on any one analysand. This is because of how we might predict he or she will idiosyncratically react to treatments of differing frequency. Since learning and change will create anxiety, we must ask whether any one analysand might react to treatment by becoming increasingly resistant because the impact of the treatment presents a narcissistic threat.

Therefore, what I think we can say is that the system has *the potential* with any one analysand to bring about chaos (i.e., the emergence of non-linearity), expressed by the emergence *into consciousness*, via interpretation, of the patterns of affect symptomatic of their strange attractors. We might go further and hypothesise that the inevitable disturbance brought about by the iterating quality of the psychoanalytic procedure creates the conditions for anxiety and regression and, thus, dependency on the psychoanalyst. From this situation would come attachment and transference and all the other more familiar descriptions of the psychoanalytic experience for both psychoanalyst and analysand.

What are the benefits of increased frequency of sessions? Etchegoyen (1991), as we will see below, indicated that he could not establish a psychoanalytic process at frequencies fewer than four times per week, although he acknowledged that many analysts seemed to manage it. I think it might be said that what is gained is the readier identification of the strange attractors governing an analysand's psychic life as they emerge as a reaction to the increasing frequency of iteration. This is the product of the psychoanalytical procedure and the psychoanalytical process it promotes. Further, we can see that, in addition to being a cognitive experience, increasing frequency will have the potential for the experience to become a directly emotional one.

There is a link with Etchegoyen's (1991) experience in which he says,

> It is very difficult for me to establish a real psychoanalytic contact with a rhythm of three times per week, although I know many analysts manage it. The number five—beyond the many symbolisms that can be interpreted—seems to me to be the most adequate, because it establishes a substantial period of contact and a clear break at the weekend. A rhythm as inconsistent as and alternating as an analysis every other day does not, in my opinion, enable the conflict of contact and separation to arise with sufficient strength. The treatments of one or two sessions per week do not generally constitute a psychoanalytic process, although it may be called that. I am inclined to believe that these cases the analyst believes, undoubtedly in good faith, that he is

carrying out an analysis. But the process exhibits the characteristics of psychotherapy, that is dispersion or omission of the transference, manifest or latent reassurance formulated as interpretation, neglect of separation anxiety which is conventionally interpreted or not interpreted at all, and so forth. (p. 513)

From the passage above, we can see that Etchegoyen is using a model emphasising iterative contact and separation. From my own experience, I find that something seems to happen at frequencies of treatment at three or more times per week that is qualitatively different from fewer frequencies. It is hard to specify exactly what it is. We can make use of phenomenological distinctions to explain this qualitative change. For example, we might say there is a different kind of free association that becomes freer over a period of time because both participants in the system feel a greater familiarity and trust. I think there is also a way in which each session ends in an incomplete manner, leaving *nachtraglichkeit* to do its work. However, regardless of the manner in which we might find a resonance in Etchegoyen's words with our own experiences, I think we do need some kind of model that is capable of convincing those outside the field without our experience. The trouble with confining our thoughts to assuming that increased frequency leads to the establishment of a psychoanalytic process is that, while it may satisfy those who work at frequencies of four to five times per week, it will not convince others who work at a lower frequency but who, none the less, think they are establishing a psychoanalytical process. Etchegoyen, indeed, recognises this.

In practical terms, I think we can now see the importance of "gauging the dose" and some of the factors that go into making such a choice. If this is the case, then it seems to me that the profession needs to develop more articulated views on precisely how the frequency of sessions per week has an effect on the quality of the psychoanalytic experience. At present, it seems that we recognise that it has such an effect in general terms based on our professional experience. However, I think that the direct implication of the ideas I have been putting forward in this chapter is that, in the assessment of potential patients, the frequency of sessions needs to be considered explicitly in relation to the balance of the forecast propensity for learning and the anticipated resistance. Further, in the training of psychoanalysts, the opportunity should be provided to learn about the impact upon psychoanalytic learning of differing frequencies of treating per week.

In conclusion

At the start of this chapter, I said that I wanted to explore the hypothesis that the psychoanalytical procedure, in and of itself, has the property of disturbing an analysand's psychic structures. At its most basic, my initial conclusion is that, because our experience is that varying the number of sessions per week has a powerful impact on a psychoanalytical treatment, what we offer a patient means that this aspect of the setting is not therapeutically inert. In practice, it has a powerful impact, independent of the content of the analysis, on the effectiveness of the psychoanalytic treatment.

In the course of this exploration, I have posited the idea that this procedure creates an iterative learning system. All iterative systems have the property of manifesting unpredictable variations in their output relative to their input in certain situations. What predicts the output is not just the input, but also the conditions (or, in more common psychoanalytic terms, the setting) in which the transformation of input into output occur.

During a psychoanalysis, we can see how an analysand's psychic structure is revealed when what is seen over a period of months is replicated in the course of a session. Thus, a structure gradually emerges which manifests varying forms but, in essence, remains similar in structure. This reveals the presence of fixations, internal objects, or unconscious phantasies which function as strange attractors, essentially and unconsciously maintaining the coherence of that analysand's psychic system. The structure will be seen in the analysand's history, his conception of his history and future, and in the "here and now" of the transference. Therefore, we arrive *at a hypothesis* that variations in the value of *a* (one aspect of which is the frequency of sessions per week) of the algorithm governing the iterative process of the psychoanalytical procedure will predict the emergence of these strange attractors and, hence, the ease with which they can be observed.

The implication is that the effect of increasing the number of sessions per week is not predictable in a *simple additive way*. Thinking of this in an arithmetically additive manner implies that two sessions are twice as good as one and five sessions are five times as effective. What we seem to have developed is a hypothesis that the impact of increasing the number of sessions per week is determined by the value of *a* in the algorithm determining the iterative learning system for any one patient. The impact is counterbalanced by the effect of b, which is partly dependent on the value of a however b is to be measured. We might then be able to envisage that the impact of two sessions is greater than one and less than five without implicitly assuming that the increase must occur in an arithmetically additive way. However, I think what we can say is that increasing the value of a in the algorithm increases *the potential* of the procedure to create unpredictability and uncertainty in the analysand and, thus, regression and transference or an increase in b. It is equally clear from this conceptual model that a and b must always be present and co-exist when intervening in a complex system such as the mind. Learning must always co-exist with resistance because a complex system must maintain its integrity.

Indeed, as a result, one might propose that Freud's discovery of the psychoanalytic technique, as a means of gaining access to an analysand's internal reality, worked because he unknowingly found a way of harnessing the power of iterating learning systems implied by his innovatory technique to make contact with unconscious process through repetition and feedback. Thus, if disturbance or unpredictability apparently occur, it might not be *solely* because of how the analysand is reacting to the psychoanalyst's interpretations.

This, then, is a procedure that has the potential to be powerful in revealing psychic structure in its unconscious and affective sense and not solely in the conscious intellectual sense. There is reason to think that it becomes more powerful as the setting becomes optimal for enabling the strange attractors defining an analysand's psychic structure to reveal itself. For this reason, those being trained in its practice need experience of its full power from the point of view of being both a psychoanalyst and a patient. Put in plain terms, you do not train racing drivers by never taking them out of third gear. You will also need to be sure that they can run through the gears—top to bottom.

To conclude, my purpose in putting forward these ideas is to propose that if we think of the psychoanalytic procedure as an iterative learning system, we have a basis for beginning to understand why the number of times a patient is seen per week has the effect that we experience it having in our professional practice. However, the impact of the number of times an analysand is seen per week seems to have been overlooked in our scientific literature and, for various reasons, ranging from the scientific to the political, it seems timely to remedy this oversight. I do not think I will have provided the definitive answer to the problem in this chapter, but I hope it will begin a process leading to a satisfactory position on the matter.

There are, of course, many aspects of this approach to thinking about the setting that have yet to be explored. Therefore, I regard these thoughts as a beginning and that we need to do much work and research on understanding the operation of the iterative learning system in the settings within which we work every day. For example, the morphogenetic properties of the procedure have not been explored in this paper. However, I think it can be concluded that the frequency of sessions is a crucial aspect of the setting because of its undoubted impact on the psychoanalytical experience. By taking this effect for granted, and thus remaining essentially unaware of it, I think we miss the chance to see why the psychoanalytic experience is as powerful as it is.

Note

1.   An example of a linear equation (e.g., $y = mx + c$) is recognisable graphically as a simple straight line when plotted against two dimensions measuring, for example, an input (x) and an output (y), enabling y to be calculated from x exactly and reliably. Thus, m represents the gradient of the line defining the proportional relationship between x and y. c is a constant showing where the line crosses the y axis.

References

Britton, R. (2004). Subjectivity, objectivity and triangular space. *Psychoanalytic Quarterly*, 73: 47–61.

Etchegoyen, H. (1991). *The Fundamentals of Psychoanalytic Technique.* London: Karnac.

Fonagy, P., & Target, M. (1996). Predictors of outcome in child psychoanalysis: a retrospective study of 763 cases at the Anna Freud Centre. *Journal of the American Psychoanalytic Association*, 44: 27–77.

Freud, S. (1900a). *The Interpretation of Dreams. S. E.*, 4–5. London: Hogarth.

Freud, S. (1913c). On beginning the treatment. *S. E.*, 12: 121–144. London: Hogarth.

Galatzer-Levy, R. M. (1995). Psychoanalysis and dynamical systems theory: prediction and self similarity. *Journal of the American Psychoanalytic Association, 43*: 1085–1113.

Galatzer-Levy, R. M. (2009). Good vibrations: analytic process as coupled oscillations. *International Journal of Psychoanalysis, 90*(5): 983–1007.

Gedo, P. M., & Cohler, B. J. (1992). Session frequency, regressive intensity, and the psychoanalytic process. *Psychoanalytic Psychology, 9*: 245–249.

Gill, M. (1984). Psychoanalysis and psychotherapy: a revision. *International Review of Psycho-analysis, 11*: 161–179.

Hartocollis, P. (2003). Time and the psychoanalytic situation. *Psychoanalytic Quarterly, 72*: 939–957.

Langston, C. (1990). Computation on the edge of chaos: phase transition and emergent computation. *Physica D, 42*: 12–37.

Moran, M. G. (1991). Chaos theory and psycho-analysis. *International Review of Psycho-analysis, 18*: 211–222.

Piers, C. (2000) Character as self-organizing complexity. *Psychoanalytic Contemporary Thought, 23*: 3–34.

Piers, C. (2005). The mind's multiplicity and continuity. *Psychoanalytic Dialogues, 15*: 229–254.

Quinodoz, J.-M. (1997). Transitions in psychic structures in the light of deterministic chaos theory. *International Journal of Psychoanalysis, 78*(4): 699–718.

Siegel, S. (1956). Non-parametric statistics for the behavioural sciences. McGraw-Hill, New York.

Von Bertalanffy, L. (1950). An outline of general system theory. *British Journal for the Philosophy of Science, 1*: 134–165.

CHAPTER SEVEN

Some research implications*

Graham Shulman

Smith (2007, p. 159) states that "our best models of the world are non-linear", that "chaos has changed the goal posts" in science and that "[t]he study of chaos has provided new tools" (2007, p. 160). How might chaos theory and these "new tools" be used in research within the field of psychoanalysis or psychoanalytic psychotherapy? While conventional time series techniques and statistical methods of analysis have been used in research in child psychoanalysis or psychoanalytic child psychotherapy (e.g., Moran & Fonagy, 1987; Philps, 2009; Schneider et al., 2009), as far as I am aware, non-linear models and the "new tools" derived from chaos and dynamical systems theory have not so far been employed in psychoanalytic research. The lesson from chaos theory seems to be that statistical analysis and conventional time series techniques, while unquestionably useful in studying linear correlations and relationships, are unable to observe or identify non-linear deterministic patterns, structures, or chains of cause and effect. This means the assumption based on conventional statistical analysis of linear patterns that "[i]f . . . two

* Material from this chapter was originally published in the *Journal of Child Psychotherapy*, 36(3): 259–288 and is reproduced with permission of Taylor & Francis.

processes are uncorrelated, it is unlikely that they are causally connected" (Moran & Fonagy, 1987[2009, p. 88]) *proves to be incorrect in
relation to non-linear or chaotic processes.*

From the papers reproduced in this book, there are several areas
of research opened by the complex systems perspective. One concerns
how we think about development—psychic and physical—and how
we can understand the patterns of discontinuity that we observe in
practice. This might enable us to go a step beyond simple behavioural
observation to see the interaction between an individual's potential
that he is are born with and how this responds to the psychic and
physical impact of what he experiences as he lives. What we see are
situations, which are implicitly organisations of experience.

Measurement in research design

Marks-Tarlow (personal communication) has suggested that methods
of data analysis deriving from dynamical systems theory, chaos theory,
and complexity theory are particularly well suited to capture the
temporal aspects of clinical experience, and, more specifically, the non-
linear recurrent themes and underlying "relational attractors" that
arise over time in the clinical setting. All of these methods are based
on the use of complex and sophisticated mathematical approaches.
Tschacher and colleagues (1998) used the concept of state space for an
empirical study of order and pattern formation in psychotherapy.
Dynamical systems theory has given rise to the development and use
of state space grids (Lewis et al., 1999). A state space grid "incorporates
time as a dimension of analysis" (Hollenstein, 2007, p. 384), and
involves the representation in two-dimensional grid form of high
dimensional dynamical systems. In the field of developmental psychology, Lewis and colleagues (1999) used state space grids to study
early infant socio-emotional development, and Hollenstein (2007) has
reviewed the use of state space grids, and the associated concepts of
attractors and phase transitions, in a number of other studies that
analyse the *process* of infant and child development across time.

Another system of data analysis suited to non-linear systems
is recurrence plotting (Eckmann et al., 1987; Marwan, 2003; Marwan
et al., 2007): this is an advanced system of non-linear data analysis and
involves a method of plotting "all the times when the phase space

trajectory of the dynamical system visits roughly the same area in the phase space" (Williams, 1997). Cross recurrence plotting shows "all those times at which a state in one dynamical system occurs simultaneously in a second dynamical system", and joint recurrence plotting shows "all those times at which a recurrence in one dynamical system occurs simultaneously with a recurrence in a second dynamical system" (Williams, 1997).

A more recently developed technique is orbital decomposition (Pincus, 2001; Pincus et al., 2011). This is a complex mathematical method particularly suited to analysing patterns of change of state of a non-linear system over time, by studying and coding recurrent patterns and variations in "strings" of categorical data in a time series. Pincus and colleagues (Pincus, 2001; Pincus & Guastello, 2005; Pincus & Perez, 2006; Pincus et al., 2008) have applied this method of data analysis to the study of family and group dynamics, and more recently orbital decomposition has been used in other fields, including a study of the physician–patient relationship with patients with uncontrolled diabetes (Katerndahl & Parchman, 2010), and also in a study of violence in human societies over time (Spohn, 2008).

These techniques of data analysis of non-linear patterns and dynamics clearly require an in-depth knowledge of dynamical systems and chaos theory combined with specialist mathematical skills and knowledge. The application of chaos theory and use of such non-linear data analysis techniques within the field of psychoanalytic research would require collaborative research projects that would bring together psychoanalytic clinicians and academics with the necessary knowledge and skills. This would obviously be a considerable practical challenge.

Research into psychoanalytic process

Another area of research is into the nature of the psychoanalytic process. Galatzer-Levy's (2009) paper, in offering the concept of linked oscillators, opens up a perspective that enables a much fuller consideration of all the verbal and non-verbal factors that have an impact on the psychoanalytic experience. For example, we might think of empathy reflecting a particular kind of co-oscillation between analyst and analysand. It might help us to understand why it is that research shows that the effectiveness of psychotherapy—of whatever form—is determined by the relationship between patient and therapist.

On another level, there is the question of how and whether such theories, approaches, and techniques might be of relevance or use to the discipline of psychoanalysis and within child psychoanalytic research. I think this is an open question, and my aim has been to raise this question and, I hope, to have inspired an interest in others to explore this further. It is a commonplace clinical phenomenon to observe a *leitmotif* in, and primary organiser of, the clinical material and transference dynamics of sessions, and the presence of these in a patient's treatment (and life) is a familiar phenomenon to clinicians. The patterns of recurrence of such *leitmotifs* would appear to go hand in hand with Spence's (1987, pp. 188–189) suggestion (see below) that "the recursive structure lies at the heart of much of our experience in 'real life' and at the heart of many significant clinical phenomena". Schneider and colleagues (2009, p. 76) refer to the difficulty in research studies of identifying and capturing in data analysis "the mosaic of therapeutic patterns" and the "myriad dynamics and nuances within sessions". Authors who have employed techniques of data analysis deriving from dynamical systems theory and chaos theory have invariably concluded that *the findings of their studies could not have been reached through conventional systems of data analysis*. Within the field of psychoanalytic child psychotherapy, the case for a pluralistic research culture (Desmarais, 2007) and need for complementary research techniques (Carlberg, 2009; Philps, 2009; Schneider et al., 2009) have increasingly been highlighted. Chaos theory and the techniques of data analysis of non-linear patterns and dynamics might provide new ways of endorsing existing knowledge within the field of psychoanalysis; or they might conceivably reveal unexpected patterns, generate new hypotheses or introduce new questions.

Descriptions of ongoing experience

Although chaos theory emerged in the 1960s, the implications and applications of chaos theory in both the natural and applied sciences are still very much in the process of being discovered and elaborated. Chaos theory does not in any sense replace classical mechanistic reductionist science; rather, it identifies a distinct category of deterministic non-linear phenomena and of cause and effect in the physical and natural worlds that cannot be revealed or measured by classical science.

Writers on chaos theory (Gleick, 1987; Gribbin, 2004; Lewin, 1992; Lorenz, 1993; Smith, 2007; Williams, 1997) invariably make the point that chaos, in its scientific sense, is ubiquitous and that—contrary to classical science's Newtonian assumption of a "clockwork universe"—it now seems likely that most phenomena in the physical and natural world are, in fact, chaotic in the scientific sense. Research in the past two decades in human biology and physiology applying chaos theory techniques of analysis has revealed that patterns of heart functioning, oscillatory diseases, epilepsy, and brain functioning all demonstrate properties of chaos, as defined scientifically. As Rustin (2001) has argued, the notion of a scientific paradigm that studies non-linear changes in organisations or states of a system over time, and patterns of turbulence and perturbation, is of self-evident interest and relevance to a psychoanalytic model and description of the mind and its functioning from infancy onwards.

It can be argued that Melanie Klein anticipated some of the applications of chaos theory and significance of iteration, recursion, and narrative.

In the following extract, she says,

> the primal processes of introjection and projection lead to constant changes in the ego's relation to its objects, with fluctuations between internal and external, good and bad ones, according to the infant's phantasies and emotions as well under the impact of his actual experiences. The complexity of these fluctuations engendered by the perpetual activity of the two instincts underlies the development of the ego in relation to the external world as well as the building up of the internal world. (Klein, 1958, p. 239)

In the above extract, Klein captured a fundamental characteristic of mental life and experience *as it is lived and evolves over time* in terms of its "constant changes", "fluctuations", "perpetual activity", and "complexity". This *temporal* dimension is a defining feature of mental life, and is integral to the psychoanalytic study and model of the mind. Psychoanalysis has contributed to the observation, description, elaboration, and explanation of this core characteristic of mental life through the discovery and delineation of internal objects, unconscious fantasies and processes (including transference and countertransference), and psychic organisations. What chaos theory offers is a complementary scientific empirical methodology for studying this *non-linear* temporal aspect of mental life: that is, it offers the possibility of identifying non-linear patterns of changes of state over time.

The primary data of the psychoanalytic study of the mind is the "first-order history . . . of the analytic dialogue" (Schafer, 1981, p. 49). In psychoanalytic child psychotherapy, the conventional "standardised" form of this primary psychoanalytic data is process recording— the observational, sequential, detailed, fine-grained micro-description of speech, behaviour, feeling, action, and interaction *as they unfold over time*. One could think of the "basic unit" of this data as a process recording of a single clinical session, but the total data might cover a single session or else a series of sessions over the course of a week, a month, a term, or an entire treatment (e.g., Klein, 1961). This means that the data which are studied are, by definition, a form of *narrative*. (This kind of observational descriptive process recording narrative is to be distinguished from the autobiographical or self-analytical activity of "[c]onstructing narratives" or stories about ourselves, which Bernstein (1990, pp. 55–56) terms "narrative self-reflection", in which "we rehearse past events" that we regard as significant in our "life-history".)

In Chapter Five, I suggested that the damaged object was a psychic *leitmotif* in the psychotherapy, as in the internal world and life, of a child whom I called Isaac. Are there patterns in the recurrence of such *leitmotifs*, and in the "constant changes", "fluctuations", and "complexity" of mental life over time, that have properties of non-linearity and chaos in its scientific sense? This question is one that has been increasingly addressed in the psychoanalytic literature in the past two decades.

Levin (2000) refers to the way in which

> . . . each patient shows a consistent *signature* in their pattern of being. One could argue that this signature is fractal-like in that it reappears at various levels of "magnification" in the patient's behaviour and thinking (Galatzer-Levy, 1997). (Levin, 2000, p. 93)

Levin (2000, p. 91) suggests that "chaos theory is robust in its ability to mathematically describe developmental patterns, such as the growth of trees, snowflakes, brains or mind". The application or extension of chaos theory to fields outside mathematics and the natural sciences—such as psychology—is a matter of dispute among some scientists, and Gell-Mann (1994) bemoaned what he regarded as the misuse or corruption of the concept of chaos by literary or popular culture. Nevertheless, there has been a gradual proliferation of studies in the psychological field applying chaos theory to the understanding of mental life, some using increasingly complex and sophisticated systems of data analysis deriving from non-linear dynamical systems theory and chaos theory. These techniques of data analysis have the ability to identify "visible relationships" in non-linear systems to which "statistical analysis is blind" (Smith, 2007).

Concepts such as *iteration* and *recursion* might provide ways of linking chaos theory with ideas such as *"leitmotif"* and "signature" referred to above. In mathematics, iteration refers to the repeated application of an equation or calculation (e.g., an algorithm), where the output of one step of the process becomes the input for the next; in computer science, it refers to the repeated application of a set of instructions, again each application acting on the output of the previous one. Recursion refers to a repeated process or operation that acts upon itself, or, in a more general sense, to the process of repeating objects in a self-similar way. These concepts might offer tools for the formal study of non-linear variations of a recurrent theme or repeated dynamic in the clinical data from a psychotherapy case, in a way that does justice to the *temporal* characteristic of mental life highlighted by Klein.

In addition to articles in journals, two systematic attempts to apply chaos theory to the mind and to the process of psychotherapy—both, interestingly, from the USA—are Butz's (1997) *Chaos and Complexity: Implications for Psychological Theory and Practice* and Marks-Tarlow's (2008) *Psyche's Veil: Psychotherapy, Fractals and Complexity*. Butz (1997, p. 2), a clinical psychologist and university academic, suggests that "Chaos and complexity theories represent the cutting edge of modern science", and he applies the concept of non-linearity to notions of psychological growth and development, psychopathology, personality, the self, and change. Marks-Tarlow (2008, p. 3), a practising psychotherapist in the USA and a Research Associate at the Institute of Fractal Research in Kassel, Germany, similarly argues that "Non-linear dynamics represents the science of change". She makes links between chaos and complexity theory, neuroscience research, psychological and psychoanalytic models of the mind, development and change, and "coupled dynamics", where two or more dynamical systems (e.g., two minds) "share the same underlying attractors" (Marks-Tarlow, 2008, p. 58).

Within the field of literary studies, and, more specifically, in relation to the formal study of literary narrative, a number of writers would seem relevant. Rimmon-Keenan (1983: 16), in her analysis of narrative fiction, refers to the ways in which in literary narratives "*events* combine to create *micro-sequences* which in turn combine to create *macro-sequences*" (original italics). Citing the semiologist Claude Bremond (1966), Rimmon-Kenan (1983, p. 23) discusses the concept of "embedding", where "one sequence is inserted into another as a specification or detailing of one of its functions", in effect articulating the property of recursion in narrative. Interestingly, she also discusses Bremond's (1966) study of "bifurcation" in literary narratives, as well as his idea of movements in narratives toward either "equilibrium" or "disequilibrium"; bifurcation is an important concept in chaos theory related to phase-changes in the state of a dynamical system and to stages in the movement of a system towards chaos.

More recently, Parker (2007) has applied chaos theory to the study of narrative form in the novels of four novelists. In her introductory chapter, "Chaos theory and the dynamics of narrative", Parker (2007, p. 27) elaborates the notion of "chaotic narratives" and suggests that "Chaos theory . . . enables us to reevaluate iterative sequences in texts". She explores in particular the idea of strange attractors in narrative texts, and proposes that "[i]n the narrative text, the attracting point comprises motifs" (2007, p. 28). Parker finds in the texts she analyses the property of "similarity across scale . . . whereby structural similarities occur at both global and local levels", and she links this with the "scaling . . . often noted in fractal forms" (2007, p. 39). In her discussion of Sterne's *Tristram Shandy*, Parker (2007, p. 38) shows the way in which "the text serves as an implicit demonstration of the fact that *linear causality inadequately models the complex workings of the mind*" (my italics).

Non-linear conceptions of narrative

A psychoanalytic treatment can be said to seek to create a new narrative about a patient's life. Donald Spence, a psychoanalyst with an interest in links between psychoanalysis and narrative, has written about recursion in narrative and its relevance to mental life and clinical experience. In his article "Narrative recursion" (1987, pp. 188–189), Spence argues that "the recursive structure lies at the heart of much of our experience in 'real life' and at the heart of many significant clinical phenomena". Spence discusses the connections between "repetition", "pattern", "theme and variations", and the property of recursion. He suggests that in a "recursive narrative", while "our first impression may be one of random change", there is an "underlying principle which provides the repetitive pattern", and this pattern is "strictly determined" (1987, p. 190). Fascinatingly, Spence formulates the concept of the "recursive operator" which can "*completely determine* the shape of the data" (original italics) (1987, p. 190). Here, "the *extent of transformation* is defined by the underlying recursive operator" (my italics). Spence makes no reference to chaos theory and gives no indication of being aware of the concept of the "strange attractor", but his concept of the "recursive operator" seems remarkably close to that of the "strange attractor", including the way in which a strange attractor fully determines the possible trajectory (i.e., "extent of transformation") of a dynamical system in state space.

Spence elucidates the "reasons why recursive narratives have a particular relevance to clinical observations" (1987, p. 190). First, he points to the way in which "a recursive operator can generate a complex universe of data points". Second, he makes the link between an "underlying recursive operator" and "an unconscious phantasy or early memory" (1987, p. 191). Third, he draws attention to the "resemblance between recursion and clinical repetition—in particular, repetition in the transference" (p. 191): the "variations on a . . . theme" that are observed in the transference are, Spence argues, "not casual or quixotic but, quite the contrary, tightly controlled and overdetermined" (p. 191). Spence considers different types of recursion in the clinical setting, such as when "language becomes action [in the transference] and content becomes form" (1987, p. 194), and he suggests that "[t]he transition from language to action is a special property of clinical recursion and one reason why the underlying operator . . . is often hard to identify" (1987, p. 195).

Spence illustrates the action of a recursive operator in the clinical setting through a discussion of the role of interpretation in shaping the pattern of clinical data over time. Discussing the question of methodological validity in psychoanalytic interpretation, he argues that "the recursive operator and the opportunity for repeated confirmations is significantly more convincing than the more usual procedure of using the patient's associations to validate an interpretation" (Spence, 1987, p. 201)

Last, he speculates that "Future investigations of recursive narratives may well reveal *typical time patterns* which can be used to further support the assumption of an underlying recursive operator" (Spence, 1987, p. 202, my emphasis).

This brings us full circle to the question of the possible research applications of chaos theory and the study of deterministic non-linear (chaotic) time patterns in relation to clinical material. A recent and original attempt to apply the paradigm of complexity within the context of psychoanalytic research is that of Lush's article, "Clinical facts, turning points and complexity theory" (2011). Lush discusses the debate about the relationship between clinical facts and scientific facts, and the issue of the place of subjectivity and objectivity in clinical practice, which, in turn, links with the question of the "data problem" in clinical research. She highlights the significance of the "choice of unit for analysis", and—like Galatzer-Levy—considers how we might "understand the relationship between processes revealed through detailed analysis of a single session and change over the whole period" of treatment (2011, p. 43). Lush argues that "[t]here are many ideas from complexity theory that would seem to link naturally with the process of psychoanalysis", and elaborates on why the concept of the strange attractor is particularly relevant to "a research method that takes as its starting point a single session". Lush proposes more generally that complexity theory represents "a paradigm which is helpful in thinking about the ordering patterns within complex multi-dimensional systems including patterns of psychic order" (2011, p. 45).

Another, more recent, original and innovative use of complexity theory within psychoanalytic child psychotherapy research is Coyle's (2015) study of the processes of change in psychoanalytic psychotherapy. Coyle was interested in the relationship between psychoanalysis and complexity theories, and whether complexity theory can provide a meta-framework capable of triangulating findings discovered in psychoanalytic, clinically based research. Coyle draws on concepts from complexity theory and features of complex dynamical systems to inform the identification and tracking of periods of change longitudinally. The research study focuses on tracking a single variable across a data set contextualised within the trajectory of a complex dynamical system. Coyle studied a child's use of Hide and Seek, and variants of this game, in psychotherapy sessions as a meaningful indicator of fluctuations, changes, and developments in emotional states of mind and internal object relations. The incidence and recurrence of various sub-types of Hide and Seek play were tracked over the entire treatment, which lasted more than two years. Coyle developed her own method of data analysis in order to produce incidence charts for the sub-types of Hide and Seek play, consistent with the technique of recurrence plotting mentioned earlier. These incidence/recurrence charts and the findings of the research study identified non-linear trajectories and patterns of change with fractal properties. A further finding was that of self-similar phenomena which were identifiable over two levels of abstraction. This original research study points the way for future possibilities in psychoanalytic, clinically based research that applies complexity theory to the psychoanalytic process.

What is apparent is the clear difference in the research methodologies used in the development of theory and practice used by those interested in behaviour from research methodologies used by those interested in experience. Different methodologies can be expected to produce different sorts of conclusions and, in so doing, create different conceptualisations of what it is that they study. However, to achieve what is advocated by Whittle is easier said than done. He says that the two camps regard each other in disbelief and ask, "How can you think like that?" We might wonder whether the tension between these views reflects a conceptual debate and conflict reaching from psychology to philosophy and beyond.

Acknowledgements

I am very grateful to Terry Marks-Tarlow for bringing to my attention information and articles regarding the use of state space grids, recurrence plotting, and orbital decomposition methods of data analysis.

References

Bernstein, J. M. (1990). Self-knowledge as praxis: narrative and narration in psychoanalysis. In: *Narrative in Culture: The Uses of Storytelling in the Sciences, Philosophy and Literature* (pp. 51–80). London: Routledge.

Bremond, C. (1966). La logique des possibles narratifs. *Communications, 8*: 60–76.

Butz, M. R. (1997). *Chaos and Complexity: Implications for Psychological Theory and Practice.* Bristol, PA: Taylor & Francis.

Carlberg, G. (2009). Exploring change process in psychodynamic child psychotherapy: the therapist's perspective. In: N. Midgley, A. Anderson, E. Grainger, T. Nesic-Vukovic, & K. Urwin (Eds.), *Child Psychotherapy and Research: New Approaches, Emerging Findings* (pp. 100–112). London: Routledge.

Coyle, A.-M. (2015). The complex world of hide and seek: Investigations into the use and meaning of hide and seek play and how it is related to processes of change within a looked after boy engaged in psychoanalytic psychotherapy. Doctoral Thesis for UEL/Tavistock Clinic Professional Doctorate in Psychoanalytic Psychotherapy with Children, Adolescents and their Families. Unpublished.

Desmarais, S. (2007). Hard science, thin air and unexpected guests: a pluralistic model of rationality, knowledge and conjecture in child psychotherapy research. *Journal of Child Psychotherapy, 33*(3): 283–307.

Eckmann, J. P., Kamphorst, S. O., & Ruelle, D. (1987). Recurrence plots of dynamical systems. *Europhysics Letters, 5*: 973–977.

Galatzer-Levy, R. (2009). Good vibrations: a non-linear dynamical systems model of the action of psychoanalysis. *International Journal of Psychoanalysis, 90*: 983–1007.

Gell-Mann, M. (1994). *The Quark and the Jaguar: Adventures in the Simple and the Complex.* New York: W. H. Freeman.

Gleick, J. (1987). *Chaos: Making a New Science.* New York: Penguin.

Gribbin, J. (2004). *Deep Simplicity: Chaos, Complexity and the Emergence of Life.* London: Penguin.

Hollenstein, T. (2007). State space grids: analysing dynamics across development. *International Journal of Behavioural Development, 31*(4): 384–396.

Katerndahl, D., & Parchman, L. (2010). Dynamical difference in patient encounters involving uncontrolled diabetes: an orbital decomposition analysis. *Journal of Evaluation in Clinical Practice, 16*(1): 211–219.

Klein, M. (1958). On the development of mental functioning. In: *Envy and Gratitude* (pp. 236–246). London: Hogarth, 1975.

Klein, M. (1961). *Narrative of a Child Analysis*. London: Hogarth.

Levin, F. M. (2000). Learning, development and psychopathology: applying chaos theory to psychoanalysis. *Annual of Psychoanalysis, 28*: 85–104.

Lewin, R. (1992). *Complexity: Life at the Edge of Chaos*. Chicago: University of Chicago Press.

Lewis, M. D., Lamey, A. V., & Douglas, L. (1999). A new dynamic systems method for the analysis of early socioemotional development. *Developmental Science, 2*(4): 457–475.

Lorenz, E. N. (1993). *The Essence of Chaos*. Seattle: University of Washington Press.

Lush, M. (2011). Clinical facts, turning points and complexity theory. *Journal of Child Psychotherapy, 37*(1): 31–51.

Marks-Tarlow, T. (2008). *Psyche's Veil: Psychotherapy, Fractals and Complexity*. London: Routledge.

Marwan, N. (2003). Encounters with neighbours: current developments of concepts based on recurrence plots and their applications. PhD Thesis, University of Potsdam.

Marwan, N., Romano, M. C., Thiel, M., & Kurths, J. (2007). Recurrence plots for the analysis of complex systems. *Physic Reports, 438*(5–6): 237–329.

Moran, G., & Fonagy, P. (1987). Psychoanalysis and diabetic control: a single-case study. *British Journal of Medical Psychology, 60*: 357–372. Reprinted in N. Midgley, A. Anderson, E. Grainger, T. Nesic-Vukovic, & K. Urwin (Eds.), *Child Psychotherapy and Research: New Approaches, Emerging Findings* (pp. 85–99). London: Routledge, 2009.

Parker, J. A. (2007). *Narrative Form and Chaos Theory in Sterne, Proust, Woolf and Faulkner*. New York: Palgrave Macmillan.

Philps, J. (2009). Mapping process in child psychotherapy: steps towards drafting a new method for evaluating psychoanalytic case studies. In: N. Midgley, A. Anderson, E. Grainger, T. Nesic-Vukovic, & K. Urwin (Eds.), *Child Psychotherapy and Research: New Approaches, Emerging Findings* (pp. 56–71). London: Routledge.

Pincus, D. (2001). A framework and methodology for the study of non-linear, self-organizing family dynamics. *Non-linear Dynamics, Psychology and Life Sciences, 5*(2): 139–174.

Pincus, D., & Guastello, S. J. (2005). Non-linear dynamics and interpersonal correlates of verbal turn-taking patterns in group therapy. *Small Group Research, 36*(6): 635–677.

Pincus, D., & Perez, K. (2006). Orbital decomposition for analyzing conversation patterns: an example using contiguous family therapy sessions. Workshop at the Annual Meeting of the Society for Chaos Theory in Psychology and Life Sciences, Johns Hopkins University, Baltimore, MD.

Pincus, D., Fox, K. M., Perez, K. A., Turner, J. S., & McGeehan, A. R. (2008). Non-linear dynamics of individual and interpersonal conflict in an experimental group. *Small Group Research, 39*(2): 150–178.

Pincus, D., Ortega, D. L., & Metten, A. M. (2011). Orbital decomposition for multiple time-series comparisons. In: S. J. Guastello & R. A. M. Gregson (Eds.), *Non-linear Dynamical Systems Analysis for the Behavioral Sciences: Real Data* (pp. 517–538). Boca Raton, FL: CRC Press/Taylor & Francis.

Rimmon-Kenan, S. (1983). *Narrative Fiction: Contemporary Poetics.* London: Methuen.

Rustin, M. J. (2001). Looking in the right place: complexity theory, psychoanalysis and infant observation. *International Journal of Infant Observation, 5*(1): 122–144. Reprinted in A. Briggs (Ed.), *Surviving Space: Papers on Infant Observation* (pp. 256–278). London: Karnac, 2002.

Schafer, R. (1981). Narration in the psychoanalytic dialogue. In: W. J. T. Mitchell (Ed.), *On Narrative* (pp. 25–50). Chicago, IL: University of Chicago Press.

Schneider, C., Pruetzel-Thomas, A., & Midgley, N. (2009). Discovering new ways of seeing and speaking about psychotherapy process: the Child Psychotherapy Q-Set. In: N. Midgley, A. Anderson, E. Grainger, T. Nesic-Vukovic, & K. Urwin (Eds.), *Child Psychotherapy and Research: New Approaches, Emerging Findings* (pp. 72–84). London: Routledge.

Smith, L. (2007). *Chaos: A Very Short Introduction.* Oxford: Oxford University Press.

Spence, D. (1987). Narrative recursion. In: S. Rimmon-Kenan (Ed.), *Discourse in Psychoanalysis and Literature* (pp. 188–210). London: Methuen.

Spohn, M. (2008). Violent societies: an application of orbital decomposition to the problem of human violence. *Non-linear Dynamics, Psychology and Life Sciences, 12*(1): 1–28.

Tschacher, W., Scheier, C., & Grawe, K. (1998). Order and pattern formation in psychotherapy. *Non-linear Dynamics, Psychology and Life Sciences, 2*(3): 195–215.

Williams, G. P. (1997). *Chaos Theory Tamed.* London: Taylor & Francis.

CHAPTER EIGHT

Some clinical implications

James Rose

T he central tenet of this book is that, quintessentially, the mind is a complex system. It reacts to being studied and a linear reaction to stimulus is not to be expected, except where defined/ required as such by the assumptions of research methodology. Strange attractors give us a sense of the structure of a system which is not to do with its anatomy but how a number of different contributing factors combine in determining its functioning.

It might be proposed that the identification of the strange attractors governing an individual's behaviour and experience could provide a kind of bridge between the two camps identified by Whittle in Chapter Two. This idea of the strange attractor is central to the contributors to this book. Not only does it have theoretical and conceptual implications, it has both clinical and technical implications as well.

How might it do this? As an illustration of clinical applications, Shulman demonstrates the ways in which clinical phenomena (e.g., a damaged object) may be thought of as strange attractors (see Chapter Five). Strange attractors, however, are not to be equated with objects. There is no advantage from such an equation. If it is simply another word for the same thing, then the advantages of this approach might well be overlooked.

In Chapter Six of this book, I seek to show how the concepts derived from the theory of complex systems can be used to understand the impact of the frequency of sessions per week upon a psychoanalytic treatment. As illustrations of technical implications, he uses the ideas of Galatzer-Levy (1995), who had shown how a patient's strange attractors become manifest at what he calls different levels of magnification. These levels reflect a characteristic structure which can be observed in the "here and now" of a single session and over the history of a treatment. This is invaluable because it helps a patient to learn to observe their process; thereby enabling the split in the ego that makes it possible for that patient to use the experience within a session and apply it their life outside the session.

Thus, in addition to offering a new perspective on clinical phenomena, these ideas seem to offer a new perspective on the nature and functioning of an important aspect of the psychoanalytic setting—the number of times that analyst and patient meet together per week. The iterative learning system created by the psychoanalytic procedure can be seen to permit the observation not just of objects, but also how situations between the subject and the object are repeatedly observed. Thus, the analysand and the analyst are in a position to think and reflect on these repeated situations and the role that each party plays in them. In so far as these situations reflect the analysand's life, both analyst and analysand are in a position to observe them. This enables the analyst to disentangle the analysand from these situations and contemplate the feelings and experience that draws him into them and what the consequences are for the feelings of those who are involved in these situations. It also makes it possible for the analysand to contemplate what leads him to perceive these others in the characteristic way that he does.

If the concepts of complex systems do offer a kind of paradigm shift for those working psychoanalytically, then we can expect that some fundamental assumptions will be challenged. The impact of a paradigm shift is often to invoke a creative response in the sense of having ideas that have never before been considered. From the papers reproduced above, there are two obvious areas of research opened by the complex systems perspective. These concern how we think about time and space in the psychoanalytic learning system. What we see in the consulting room are clinical situations, which are, implicitly, organisations of experience. Because an individual's organisations of experience reflect a function that has been adaptive to the environment—be it internal or external—they will be non-linear because if they remained linear, they would quickly cease to have an adaptive property.

Turning now to the apparently irreconcilable split between the empiricists and hermeneuticists identified by Whittle, he makes the challenge that investigators of the mind should have a foot in both camps. This has a clear clinical relevance at the level of clinical technique. It also provides a basis for being able to respond to the critics of psychoanalysis for its inability to demonstrate its scientific validity. Ahumada's (2011) recent book on "Insight" explores this clinical phenomenon from a psychoanalytic point of view and an epistemological one.

In his introduction, Ahumada states that

> This book has two intertwined purposes: first, to inquire on how insight is gained in clinical psychoanalysis and, second, to clarify the epistemological place of psychoanalysis and its concepts, for which the main hurdle is the conflation of knowledge and certainty in philosophical notions of science. (Ahumada, 2011, p. 1)

Then, he considers the empiricist–hermeneutic split. The problem for the empiricist approach is that its methods of the approach to the study of the mind involve an inevitable reduction when developing measures that permit the use of conventional experimental procedure. "Subjects" and their behaviour are observed in very confined conditions. Empiricists can, therefore, be vulnerable to the criticism that they have blinded themselves to the essence of subjectivity in their efforts to measure what they observe.

The hermeneutic approach, on the other hand, is seen as concerned with interpretation of what is observed. This opens the approach to the criticism that, in making interpretation, the subjectivity of the observer is introduced and superimposed in an uncontrolled manner. It seems a split that cannot be reconciled. Each side asks the other "How can you think like that?", as suggested by Whittle in the second chapter of this book.

Ahumada then moves to a criticism of those who attack psychoanalysis on scientific/empiricist grounds. Ahumada's position is to ask how subjectivity can be reduced and measured in a manner acceptable to Grunbaum and Popper. Essentially, he feels these critics are applying a model of investigation that is inappropriate for the purpose. He suggests that they and their colleagues are being scientistic. As a result, their criticism of psychoanalysis is incapable of being a science is spurious because they assume that the appropriate method of investigation must rest on linear principles.

Both the empiricist and hermeneutic approaches are efforts to answer the question "How do/can we know?" The question then, for psychoanalysts, is how can we know and, thus, learn in the psychoanalytical learning system. Ahumada, in pursuit of this question, devotes himself to the question of insight because this offers a means of describing what is gained in the process of psychoanalytic learning. Insight is a word with the connotation of becoming aware of something new that was both unexpected and changes our understanding of our psychic reality. Accordingly, we might say that the word has validity as a means of describing part of the experience of psychoanalytic learning.

What, then, is insight and how does it occur? Ahumada takes the view that the fundamental dynamic of insight is counter-induction. This means reversing the usual logic of induction, which is to identify the general from the particular. Counter-induction is an apparently paradoxical position of taking the way things have been observed as a guide to how they are not. In essence, he feels that insight emerges as a result of the opportunity an analysand has to observe how his perception of the world is shaped by ideas (or personal theories) of which she was unaware, thereby unconscious. This enables her to see things as she did not think they were because she can see the assumptions determining their perceptions. Identification of these assumptions shaping experience is, therefore, the stuff of insight. These "ideas" might be thought to be the manifestation of the analysand's strange attractors. The concept of counter-induction arises from a logical model identified by the Finnish logician, Georg-Henryk von Wright. It seems quite counter-intuitive but can be seen as appropriate in investigating a system as complex as the human mind, part of which is unconscious. This approach permits the inclusion of the fact that the inducing subject brings to his observations all the unconscious personal theories that shape his experience. The subject's (or patient's) psychoanalyst will be using her metapsychology to create expectations of how things ought to be, which guide her interpretation of the clinical process. However, when the experience of both shows that they do not see things as they are, there is the potential for an insight for both parties. The unconscious implies the existence in the mind of thoughts and feelings, which are not allowed to be conscious, because of repression. This repression has psychic survival value for the patient. They will emerge when this repression is lifted as insight unfolds and develops.

What relevance has this for work in the consulting room? Much of this book has been concerned with the strange attractor. Repeated evidence of a particular strange attractor is demonstrated in the clinical process of treatment. This might be thought of as a clinical situation. Ahumada uses this idea, following that of Joseph (1985) describing what she called the "total situation".

In her summary of her paper, she says,

> I have tried in this paper to discuss how I think we are tending to use the concept of transference today. I have stressed the importance of seeing transference as a living relationship in which there is constant movement and change. I have indicated how everything of importance in the patient's psychic organization based on his early and habitual ways of functioning, his fantasies, impulses, defences and conflicts, will be lived out in some way in the transference. In addition, everything that the analyst is, or says, is likely to be responded to according to the patient's own psychic make-up, rather than the analyst's intentions and the meaning he gives to his interpretations. I have thus tried to discuss how the way in which our patients communicate their problems to us is frequently beyond their individual associations and beyond their words, and can often only be gauged by means of the countertransference. These are some of the points that I think we need to consider under the rubric of the total situations which are transferred from the past. (Joseph, 1985, p. 453)

It can be inferred that this emphasises that the observation and interpretation of the object relations in the *situation* of the consulting room is enriched by taking the context provided by the situation fully into account.

It might be helpful to give a clinical example of this.

A patient was characteristically late for his session but, in contrast to this, he would always say when he had to leave. In view of this repeated pattern, which both patient and I could observe, I chose initially to interpret that the patient seemed to be in two minds about coming to a session. He recognised that he wanted to come to his session—otherwise he would not be here. But, perhaps there was also another part of him that felt he did not need to come.

The patient acknowledged the existence of the antinomy of there being two parts of himself and their conflicted feelings and, further, that being late had been a feature of his life since he had been at school. I felt that this meant that he saw the situation of being late as being a characteristic of him. Consequently, it was not solely a reaction to the experience of being observed in his analysis, which might feel threatening to him.

He then observed that, while he was late for work quite often, if there was an important meeting with a client he would always be on time. Thus, it depended upon how important to him was the person he was going to meet. I commented that while he might want to give the impression that he lived in a totally atemporal space, the truth was that he was very aware of time because he always seemed to know when he had to leave to get to work. Further, his lateness perhaps confirmed that I was not very important to him. This comment brought him up short; forcing him to confront his contempt but in a way that he could not deny. After a thoughtful pause, he said that he had worked for a boss for whom he had often been late into work in his customary manner but she had constantly admonished him for his lateness. Thus, he was telling me about his experience of me as a result of his being late. He was wanting me but, at the same time, hating me because he wanted me.

He continued by saying that eventually, as they got to know each other, he found himself quite liking her, as he put it. She then stopped being such a disciplinarian. He seemed to me to have thought that he had been trying to see if she regarded him as being special to her. I put it to him that this might be the case. He said that he was quite good at that, which seemed to be, in the moment, a realisation of which he felt ashamed because it was like a kind of seduction.

It seemed to me that the situation in the consulting room had moved some way from the beginning to where we now were. At the outset, it seemed to be a face-to-face confrontation, with all its paranoid ramifications and implications. It was tempting to take up his contempt immediately, but I felt that to do so would reinforce the defences that were expressed by his being late—not to mention the defences against paranoid anxieties in general. The danger was that it would be an enactment, on my part, of the disciplinarian in his mind that he both wanted and yet hated.

So, I had chosen to wait and seek for a "helicopter" perspective on the situation so that we could analyse it from a position of observing the situation that he had created. At the time, it seemed to me that this made it possible for him to think about himself; how he acted in a manner that was essentially self-destructive; that is, he lost part of his session. We could also analyse the situation from both his own point of view and my own as he experienced it in the moment of analysing it.

He could also see the impact this might have on anyone involved in the situation. He felt it would annoy them (as it did his manager) and, in this belief, he could not see how it blinded him to seeing their concern for him. In his effort to discover whether he was especially loved, he created the very opposite: he was especially hated. I offer this vignette to illustrate how the strange attractor expressed by the repeated situation could be analysed from the overview/helicopter perspective, making it easier for him to see how he created fruitless confrontations in his mind.

I could have taken up and interpreted from the role of attacked object or the disciplinarian and sometimes it would be appropriate so to do. However, the power of the iterative psychoanalytic learning system to create the emergence of a subject's strange attractors expressing the characteristic relationships they have with their objects allows us to find a method of working that complements the "here and now" approach. It is important that these approaches are seen to complement each other. However, they come from different epistemological models. Object relations theory sees the subject relating to his objects, in the heat of moment, driven by his instinctual drives. Change results from the patient's insight into the emotional reality of their experience. Such insight, however, in practice often does not occur immediately, but it is assisted when the experience can be contemplated from a perspective outside the emotional immediacy of the patient's experience. A complex systems approach takes a longer-term view, allowing time for patterns of behaviour and experience to emerge as strange attractors—or characteristic and repeating situations—which both patient and analyst can observe and contemplate from each other's points of view. It can, therefore, be another perspective so that the patient can observe, with the help of his analyst, his experience in a different way.

A non-linear view of time

A further clinical implication arises from the question of whether it is appropriate to think about the experience of time in a linear way when considering a subjective sense of time in a repeating clinical situation. The linear model of time assumes the "arrow of time" in which the past precedes the present and is followed by the future. What happens when time is conceived from a non-linear point of view? In our culture, this may be thought of as bizarre, but the Incas had a quite different notion of time from our own linear one (Núñez & Sweetser, 2001). The Aymara word for time is the same as that for "sight", which might sound surprising to us with our linear view, but they did not make a linear assumption about time. For them, the experience of time related to what they knew (or could see)—the past and the present. We might wonder, therefore, whether the future, because they could not see it, was something that they felt they could not know. Thus, they had a sense of walking backwards into the future rather than forwards into the future, as we might think, given our linear view.

In the context of their struggle for survival, the future might only have been terrifying because it was associated with death. We might ask whether this shows that, for the Aymara speaker, the future might seem very threatening and to be avoided at all costs because it could not be seen. Maybe, the future could not be thought about because it was too frightening. The Inca society was especially concerned with the struggle for survival on a day-to-day basis. The main activity of that society seems to have been concerned with the maintenance of systems developed to ensure survival, for example, reliable food banks. They expanded their empire because they could offer these systems to the peoples that they conquered. Without a future, perhaps, the past could not be separated from the present and the individual lived in an existence where fear of death was never far from consciousness. As a result, the idea of progress might have been very difficult to contemplate. The consequence for the Inca was that when they encountered the Spanish with their linear assumption of time and, thus, the possibility of hope, ambition, and progress, they quickly succumbed. Thus, they did not survive even though this was their main concern. This is a hypothesis: we cannot know the actual personal experience of Inca time, but it might help to oil our imagination about the experience of non-linear time.

It might seem very curious to imagine what it is like to experience time in that way. However, it forces us to consider that, in any one instant in what we call the present, the past is inextricably part of the experience. This questions whether, in considering the subjective experience of time, there can be such a thing as the "here and now" which is separate from a person's history. We often notice when treating severely regressed patients that they seem to be locked in the past and cannot disentangle themselves from it. Depending on our theoretical point of view, we might regard this as a fixation or as a destructive avoidance of the "here and now" relationship with their psychoanalyst. Or, it could be that these patients are showing us the torments in which they live because they cannot separate the past from the present.

However, if they can let themselves have a history, that is, events that they can consider in retrospect, then a new situation can be achieved because they will have the capacity for a "helicopter" perspective. This is possible because the patient can see himself in the present but he can also see himself in the past and, thus, see himself from an external perspective. If the reason for this elision of past and present can be established (for example, a persistent guilt arising from a severe trauma), then the regression might dissolve because the underlying anxiety arising from this guilt can be brought to consciousness in the transference. It can be seen as having happened in the past and not being continually re-experienced in the present.

An example of this situation is given in the following.

A woman came to her psychoanalysis suffering from insomnia. She had been diagnosed as being depressed. Her history was that she had been a replacement for a boy, who had been longed for by her mother, but had died. Her father was advised to impregnate his wife as soon as possible to replace the lost child. Unfortunately, this happened before allowing time for the mother's necessary mourning. As a result, mother had not bonded to her from birth and had brought her up telling her that she was a boy. In essence, she could never be right in her mother's eyes and thus she could never have an experience of pleasing her mother. This had led to her depression and she had defended herself against this agony by cutting herself off from her feelings, which enabled her to have a life of sorts, but one empty of meaning.

In the course of a lengthy analysis, she gradually became able to experience her feelings as a woman in a woman's body. This arose from her becoming, little by little, aware of how she missed me in my absence, which she became conscious of experiencing as my ruthless rejection. This achievement brought her defences into conscious recognition, which was very frightening for her. Indeed, it threatened psychic chaos. She began to be very emphatic in her hatred of my rejection implied by my absences. This, in turn, enabled a sense of feeling emotionally "real"; which was, none the less, very frightening because it risked losing me forever. It exactly paralleled her relationship with her mother. This equation of these feelings towards her mother and myself enabled us to see how her past existed in the present in a seemingly indissoluble way. Thus, she could not allow herself to have a history to give meaning to her feelings in the present. For her to make such a step required an angry rejection *of* her mother/analyst, which, it was feared, would be certain to lead to a rejection *by* her mother/analyst. The consequence of this rejection was therefore, for her, death—psychic or physical. Thus, it was an enormous step forward to be able—or allow herself—to express her anger with me with the energy that she did.

Yet, while she understood this dilemma intellectually, it was without feeling in spite of this energy. The admission of feeling and its expression became truly terrifying because of the certainty of rejection and, thus, relegation to a frightening void. At the same time, the strength of these feelings could not be denied and she began to be very depressed, with a sense of despair because she could not see any way out of it. It seemed that it was better for her to have a terrifying mother than no mother at all. Her despair was that if she expressed rage towards her mother, she would lose her; but, if she repressed these feelings, the result would be depression.

I could see that, if she could allow herself a history, there might be a way out of her despair, but that would be much easier said than actually achieved. She knew it intellectually but she could not make the necessary shift needed to see it as something belonging to the past. This was because making the shift, subjectively, meant the loss of her mother. What was so difficult was achieving the helicopter position, which would be the result of achieving a sense of history. This situation seemed to be an impasse in which acknowledging her feelings would lead to a devastating loss. Denying her feelings would lead to depression. Thus, the question became one of how to resolve this impasse?

As it happened, many of these difficulties were expressed in a relationship with a woman with whom she had lived for many years, which people had assumed to be a lesbian one. As a result of awakening sexual feelings for me, she began to realise that she would have to distance herself from this person if she were to have a life, because the relationship with this woman exactly replicated that with her mother, as did her relationship with me in the transference. She managed to do this, but not without much anxiety and difficulty. Her anxiety was that it would kill this woman. Thus, she could have the insight but acting upon it was very problematic There can be little doubt that this was because she anticipated that this meant she would have to separate from me, which would pitch-fork her into a void that she dreaded. This was because the three situations—with mother, her co-habitee, and her analyst—were symmetrised, due to the comparable affect.

In the event, she achieved this separation but not without much help from me.

The immediate effect was that she could "see" her relationship with me in the transference. This was in a manner she had never achieved before because of the depth of feeling in her understanding, which was no longer confined to an intellectual one. It was achieved by seeing that her relationship with me was, in fact, quite different from the relation with her "partner", even though it had felt exactly the same. However, this could not be achieved until she could allow feelings to come into consciousness making it possible, thereby, to reflect upon them and see the situations as not being the same.

We can see that the idea of there being a "here and now" separate from the past was not available to this woman and the consequences had been devastating. She had lived all her life with the certainty of rejection. This had led her to repress her feelings, but the result was her depression. Therefore, it would have been a huge mistake on my part to interpret to her what might be deemed as a destructive attack upon me and the analysis, implicitly making an assumption about the linearity of her sense of time. Thus, we see how a non-linear concept of time has many implications for how we can conceive clinical situations theoretically and the consequent implications for clinical technique.

In this case, the achievement of a sense of history led to her being able to experience her analyst's absence in a much calmer and reflective way. How was this achieved? It was because she began to confront experiences in her life (i.e., her flatmate) that reflected the impasse in the transference. These impasses were to be found everywhere in her life. When she took steps to emerge from this one, she found that, contrary to her expectation that there would be a catastrophe, there was a new sense of freedom for both parties in the impasse.

In support of these ideas, in an earlier publication (Rose, 1997) I showed how a patient's assumptions about time have a profound effect on the transference situation in an analysis. I concluded that

> It seems to me that we can learn much about a patient's psychic reality and its structure if we observe their emotional impact upon us. Important clues to this will be found in the distortions of the space and time of the psychic field between us and the form that these distortions take. I think that an analyst's awareness of these distortions comes in a great variety of forms and may predominantly be felt in the countertransference, very often initially in a non-verbal manner and will take time to develop. (p. 267)

In essence, I felt that, while conscious experience will be dominated by the reality principle, unconscious experience would be under the sway of the pleasure principle. Thus, time, in the unconscious, cannot be said to take the form of "the arrow of time".

A non-linear conception of space

We can now turn to the spatial aspects of the situations, expressed by the strange attractors that emerge in an analysis. It might seem even harder to conceive non-linear space than non-linear time. If strange attractors in a patient's mind are made manifest by the emergence of characteristic and repeating situations in the transference, then these situations imply both time and space. Objects of fractional dimensions (or fractals) might seem beyond imaginative conception for the non-mathematician.

If we now consider the man, introduced above, who was characteristically late for his session, we could eventually see that, in his quest to discover if he was special, the effect was that he turned his good objects into persecuting ones. As his treatment continued, it emerged that something in him prevented him from pursuing any initiative to a satisfactory conclusion. This affected him in both his professional and sexual life. When he began his treatment, for example, he found it difficult to achieve an erection. This meant that he could not experience a satisfactory orgasm either himself or give such an experience to his partner.

A curious feature was that, although he seemed to fall deliberately short of what were ostensibly his hopes, he needed someone who would tell him that he had the potential to achieve what he wanted, that is, that he was special. It was almost as if his motto was "Better to travel with the hope that someone thinks I am special rather than actually to succeed". This motto, of course, was reflected his lateness to his sessions. Thus, for him, it was better to have an awareness that someone (me) was aware of his absence, than for him to be present with me and me with him. We might conceive this as a situation in which he sought to control his experience of dependency by the denial of his dependency, which was expressed by being late, but it could also imply that he was dependent on something absent. We tend to think of dependency being upon something present. What happens when this present is absent? This implied that his lateness was an enactment of some kind concerning something or someone absent. There was something very controlling which was present in its absence.

The presence of something in its absence might seem to imply loss. This arises from the notion that dependence is, or has been, upon something, or someone, present. What can happen when the dependence is upon someone who is very absent in his or her presence? André Green's concept of the dead mother describes this situation vividly. He calls the situation a complex, which is made up of the child, his mother, and whatever it is that preoccupies her.

Presence and absence might seem to be mutually exclusive but we see from Green's formulation that presence and absence can not only co-exist but that each implies the other to the child with such a mother. This has led his theorising to the notion of "the work of the negative" and the negative hallucination, which is the representation of an absence. This suggests that the situation implied by a strange attractor in psychic space entails a space encompassing a presence and absence, which are not mutually exclusive. Note that "negative" here has nothing to do with destructiveness; it is a necessary consequence of the active nature of perception. In health, it cannot *not* happen (the double negative perhaps captures its paradoxical nature to our minds).

In his paper "The dead mother", Green (1986) proposes that, in health, the child reacts to the continuing presence and absence of the mother by creating what he called a negative hallucination, which represents the presence of the mother in her absence from the child. This, he suggests, creates what he calls a *"structure encadrante"* which provides a framework for experiencing. In other words, it makes it possible to separate experience from the self. This means achieving the helicopter vision, permitting observation of the self. If this does not occur, the fate of the child is to be continually flooded by an un-differentiated experience in which she lives all the time.

When we recall a patient saying to Winnicott that his absence was more real than his presence, we get a sense of what Green envisaged the function of the negative hallucination to be. It provides a basis for the continuity of experience and, without it, the self will be flooded by experience in which there is no sense of the present being separate from the past or, indeed, the future. We can see a clear link with the various thoughts on time that were set out above. A strange attractor is not a negative hallucination, but a pattern of behaviour and associ-ated affect which can be discerned over time. The space within it does not imply just presence, but also absence—or the negative (in Green's terms) of presence.

In clinical practice, we constantly encounter in the transference a sense of the patient's history being in the present. Indeed, we might say that this is the essence of transference. What brings the past into the present is the power of affect and the need of the patient to make sense of it. In severely regressed patients, as suggested above, we can have a sense that they live in the past and cannot separate it from the present. Freud felt that hysterical patients were victims of their remi-niscences. In other words, they did not remember their histories but lived in their histories as if they were in the present, which, for them, they indeed were.

We can, therefore, propose that within the strange attractor there is a sense of space that comprises presences and absences. This cannot be avoided but it makes the notion of a sense of the present being, self-evidently, separate from history questionable; an illusion brought about by an assumption of the linearity of time. This complicates our conception of a situation because temporal dimension will not necessarily be linear. We have, therefore, seen that the non-linear view enables us to see that space and time necessarily entail an implication that, in psychic reality, past and present are intertwined, as are presence and absence. This pair of antinomies allows us to use Ahumada's concept of counter-induction because we are not forced to make implicit assumptions about a person's psychic reality based upon a linear view of that reality. These are some of the clinical implication of the non-linear approach.

References

Ahumada, J. L. (2011). *Insight: Essays on Psychoanalytic Knowing*. London: Routledge.

Green, A. (1986). *The Dead Mother*. In: *On Private Madness*. London: Hogarth Press and Institute of Psychoanalysis.

Joseph, B. (1985). Transference: the total situation. *International Journal of Psychoanalysis, 66*: 447–454.

Núñez, R., & Sweetser, E. (2001). Spatial embodiment of temporal metaphors in Aymara: Blending source-domain gesture with speech. In: Abstracts from the 7th International Cognitive Linguistics Conference (pp. 249–250). Santa Barbara: University of California, Santa Barbara.

Rose, J. S. (1997). Distortions of time in the transference. *International Journal of Psychoanalysis, 78*: 453–468.

CHAPTER NINE

Some conclusions

James Rose & Graham Shulman

O verall, this book seeks to make the case that we must accept that the mind does not work in a simple linear way. The papers produced in this book have looked at various ways in which the ideas derived from chaos theory can be used to think about clinical phenomena; how they can have technical implications for thinking about how psychoanalysts work and why the psychoanalytic method has the impact that we observe it does in practice. A central idea has been that of the strange attractor observed in the functioning of a complex non-linear dynamic system. This has implications for psychoanalysis because it gives rise to a new model for understanding psychic reality. Further, it gives us a means of understanding how the psychoanalytic method reveals this structure of psychic reality.

In summary, the new perspectives of a complex systems approach to the understanding of the psychoanalytic process can be summarised as:

1. That the mind should be seen as a non-linear system that cannot be studied by methods assuming linearity. This enables psychoanalysts to counter the critics of psychoanalysis, because these critics assume that satisfactory methods of investigation must rest on linearity.

2.   That a complex systems model gives us an understanding of why the psychoanalytic method of investigation, developed by Freud, which is based on free association, gives us a means of studying the non-linear mind. It is, as it were, "fit for purpose".

3.   Seeing complex systems as essentially iterative, with strange attractors being revealed by this iteration, emphasises a new view of the temporal dimension, perhaps changing currently prevailing ideas about clinical technique.

4.   This means of investigation enables us to observe the strange attractors governing a patient's psychic reality. These can be observed as patterns that constantly repeat. These should not be seen as repetition compulsions, which have the purpose of defence, but the reasons why psychic reality can seem to be at odds with external reality. This is because these strange attractors reflect the unconscious theories about relationships, in their presence and their absence, in particular situations. Thus, the focus of study in the consulting room is expanded to include a context, within which relations between a patient and their analyst can be observed.

5.   Taking the mind to be a non-linear system opens new avenues of research which can be supported by newly emerging statistical methods. Furthermore, we can examine our current theories by asking whether an assumption of linearity distorts our perception of the workings of the mind. We might find that this assumption leads us to ask the wrong questions, use the wrong methods, and, thus, derive mistaken conclusions.

This book is part of a series called "Psychoanalytic Ideas". How the reader of this book responds to the ideas in this book will be an experience unique to each individual and will be unquestionably subjective. If it stimulates the reader to some new ideas, it will have achieved its purpose.

INDEX